W9-CTJ-812

"THE TAROT'S ORIGINS ARE LOST IN THE MISTS OF TIME. Authorities have attributed them to the esoteric schools of philosophy of ancient Egypt or India. They were used by the Gypsies around the shores of the Mediterranean for fortune-telling long before they were rediscovered by the Renaissance schools, which were at that time also delving into the mysteries of Alchemy and the Kabalah. There was a revival of interest in the Tarot about the middle of the nineteenth century, and this has continued ever since, with scholars discovering ever new meanings, and writers using the mystifying powers of the cards as a basis for stories, poems, and plays."

—EDEN GRAY, *Mastering The Tarot*

⊘ SIGNET BOOKS

MYSTERIES OF THE OCCULT

(0451)

☐ **THE COMPLETE ART OF WITCHCRAFT by Sybil Leek.** Sybil Leek, the world's best-known witch, astounding seer, medium, astrologer and high priestess in the oldest cult known, gives the inside story on what goes on among those who live, practice and believe in a magic unknown to most of us. (127145—$2.95)*

☐ **THE COMPLETE BOOK OF MAGIC AND WITCHCRAFT by Kathryn Paulsen.** An up-to-date practitioner's manual of magic, witchcraft and sorcery—with all the ancient and modern recipes, spells, and incantations essential to the Black Arts! (137361—$3.95)*

☐ **MASTERING THE TAROT: Basic Lessons in an Ancient, Mystic Art by Eden Gray.** This book provides simple, step-by-step instructions for laying out cards and reading them as well as a precise glossary of symbols. Fully illustrated. (137191—$3.95)*

☐ **THE SEXUAL KEY TO THE TAROT by Theodor Laurence.** Let the strange and beautiful symbols of the Tarot reveal your path to gratifying love and sexual fulfillment. (119622—$2.50)

☐ **THE TAROT REVEALED: A Modern Guide to Reading the Tarot Cards by Eden Gray.** A fascinating and authoritative introduction to the ancient art of the Tarot cards. (137000—$3.95)*

*Prices slightly higher in Canada

Buy them at your local bookstore or use this convenient coupon for ordering.

NEW AMERICAN LIBRARY,
P.O. Box 999, Bergenfield, New Jersey 07621

Please send me the books I have checked above. I am enclosing $_____ (please add $1.00 to this order to cover postage and handling). Send check or money order—no cash or C.O.D.'s. Prices and numbers are subject to change without notice.

Name_____

Address_____

City_____ State_____ Zip Code_____

Allow 4-6 weeks for delivery.
This offer is subject to withdrawal without notice.

MASTERING THE
TAROT

Basic Lessons
in an Ancient, Mystic Art

EDEN GRAY

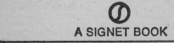

A SIGNET BOOK

NEW AMERICAN LIBRARY

© 1971 by Eden Gray

All rights reserved. No part of this book
may be reproduced or utilized in any form
or by any means, electronic or mechanical,
including photocopying, recording, or by
any information storage and retrieval system,
without permission in writing from the
Publisher. Inquiries should be addressed to
Crown Publishers, Inc., 1 Park Avenue,
New York, New York 10016.

This is an authorized reprint of
a hardcover edition published by
Crown Publishers, Inc.

SIGNET TRADEMARK REG. U.S. PAT. OFF. AND FOREIGN COUNTRIES
REGISTERED TRADEMARK—MARCA REGISTRADA
HECHO EN CHICAGO, U.S.A.

SIGNET, SIGNET CLASSIC, MENTOR, PLUME, MERIDIAN AND NAL
BOOKS *are published by New American Library*
1633 Broadway, New York, New York 10019

First Signet Printing, June, 1973

15   16   17   18   19   20   21   22   23

PRINTED IN THE UNITED STATES OF AMERICA

ACKNOWLEDGMENTS

My deep appreciation to Nan Braymer
for her invaluable assistance in the
preparation of the manuscript of this book.

Also to Mary Beckwith Cohen
for her advice on all matters that concerned Astrology,
and to Peter Gray Cohen, who made the diagrams.

CONTENTS

MASTERING THE
TAROT

GETTING ACQUAINTED
WITH THE CARDS

There is something about the Tarot that is truly fascinating. Not only do the symbols depicted on the cards challenge the imagination, but the cards themselves seem to have the power to help us explore the past and reveal hidden passions, old loves and hurts, as well as hopes and desires for the future. When you have mastered their secrets, they can give you glimpses into the future and guide you to paths that may lead to greater fulfillment.

The Tarot is not a child's game to be played and then tossed aside. Its philosophy is illuminating, and years of study do not exhaust its charm and mystery.

I myself, who am inclined to be skeptical and hard-headed, have been surprised time and again by the Tarot as it went straight to the root of a matter, picked up salient characteristics, and showed the way to a concrete solution. If the cards say there will be a delay in one's affairs when a delay does not seem possible, then delay it turns out to be. If the cards point to a girl in a young man's life, he may swear he does not know her, only to say later that she was right there at the center of the matter.

I am grateful that the cards do not predict death and only hint at illness, but they are generous with their advice, pointing almost invariably to the good, the reasonable, and even the spiritual way to accomplish one's aims.

The Tarot's origins are lost in the mists of time. Authorities have attributed them to the esoteric schools of philosophy of ancient Egypt or India. They were used by the Gypsies around the shores of the Mediterranean for fortune-telling long before they were rediscovered by the Renaissance schools, which were at that time also delving into the mysteries of Alchemy and the Kabalah. There was a revival of interest in the Tarot about the middle of the nineteenth century, and this has continued ever since, with scholars discovering ever new meanings, and writers using the mystifying powers of the cards as a basis for stories, poems, and plays.

I have been studying the Tarot for over fifteen years, and I still find the cards and their predictions a source of constant amazement. I can recall many instances in which they have helped people whose futures lay blank before them. I have seen readings give new courage to those who were dispirited or depressed. The special value of the Tarot, however, is to make people think, to weigh the pros and cons of a situation, and then to counsel the best course of action.

I recall the experience of a young man who had been out of work for some months and was offered a job that would take him out of the country. This would mean leaving his hometown, where he knew everyone, and also leaving his sweetheart. Would she wait for him? He would be gone for at least a year. A reading of the cards showed that this job was a fine opportunity and that he should take advantage of it. If he did, the cards suggested, he would find another girl more suited to him. After some hesitation, he accepted the reading and went overseas, full of anticipation for the adventures that lay before him. A postcard some months later informed me he was thoroughly enjoying his new job, was to be promoted soon, and had already found the girl the Tarot had predicted.

The Tarot deck contains seventy-eight cards, somewhat larger than our own playing cards and with altogether different meanings and powers. The very names of the two sections of the pack—the Minor and the Major Arcana— suggest their ancient and occult nature. (Arcana is the Latin word for secrets, mysteries.)

The cards illustrated in this book, which come from the Rider pack, are followed by text descriptions. In the Tarot classes I conducted for several years in New York, I always preferred this pack, designed by A. E. Waite, a renowned scholar in Alchemy, Astrology, and the occult. The designs were made under his direction by an artist highly esteemed in that day, Pamela Colman Smith. If you look closely, you will see her initials in the right-hand corner of each card.

Our minds have a way of working best by association. We find it hard to recognize new objects or ideas unless we can relate them to something we already know. Every department of our lives has a vocabulary of its own—sports, games, skills, scientific knowledge, and so on. Here you will be learning the words of a new vocabulary, but they are simple and you will soon master them as you follow the lessons.

Lesson 1

PRELIMINARY STEPS

Preparation: Open a card table or clean off a large-enough space on your dining-room table to lay out the cards without crowding them.

Shuffle the cards thoroughly. At first they may seem too large, but you will soon get used to their size and find them easy to handle.

Now turn the pack face up and, taking one after another off the top, place them in piles according to their suits. See how quickly you can put them into five piles: four for the Minor Arcana—Wands, Cups, Swords, and Pentacles—and the fifth for the Major Arcana, which are readily recognizable because each of them bears its own name beneath the picture. For the present, it is not necessary to put them in numerical order.

Each of the four suits of the Minor Arcana has cards numbered from ace to ten, followed by four court cards—Page, Knight, Queen, and King (one more than modern playing cards).

The Three of Pentacles may give you a momentary doubt, since the pentacles are hidden in the top of the arch. A sculptor stands below, looking toward a priest and a nun.

Some may be confused by the Major Arcana card Temperance, in which an angel is seen pouring water from one cup to another. This card does not belong to the suit of Cups, as you will see by the word "Temperance" at the bottom of the card. After you have sorted the cards into five piles, pick them up and shuffle them again.

A Word About Roman Numerals: Here is a quick review of Roman numerals, which are used on all the Tarot cards. Though you probably studied them in school, you may have become rusty—but you need to be able to distinguish them at a glance. The Roman symbols now commonly used are:

I—1	C—100
V—5	D—500
X—10	M—1,000

All other numbers are formed by a combination of these symbols. Thus, 6 is VI, 4 is IV, 18 is XVIII, and 19 is XIX. The capital letter *before* one larger in value is subtracted from it (IV); if a letter of *less* value *follows* (rather than precedes), it is added (VI). Here, for example, is 1390, the date attributed to the first-known Tarot cards (now on view in a European museum): MCCCXC.

Sorting: Now that you have reshuffled your cards so that they are well mixed, try sorting them again, but this time, with your memory of Roman numerals refreshed, put each suit in numerical order starting with the ace; do the same with the Major Arcana, starting with the Fool (No. 0), then I, II, and so forth. Sorting is not only good practice, but it helps you learn to distinguish a card at a glance. You might do this each time you sit down with the cards until you are really sure of their placement.

Care of the Cards: In some mysterious way, the Tarot cards seem to be influenced by the vibrations of those who handle them. People with a proper respect for their divinatory powers are usually able to get good results when laying out the cards, but those who treat the Tarot like a game may well find that the cards sometimes balk at making any sense.

The careful owner of a pack of Tarot cards protects it as much as possible. When not in use, the cards can be protected from outside vibrations by keeping them in a separate little box or wrapped up in a piece of silk. To get your cards in tune with you, or to tune them again after they have been idle for a while, try sleeping with them under your pillow for a few nights. Some people like to hold their cards quietly before they use them.

Very particular people often will not let anyone else handle their cards at all, preferring that the person for whom they read (called the Seeker) simply lay his hands on them as he thinks of his question. Then the Reader does the shuffling.

Symbols: Symbols are often used in daily life as shortcuts to more complicated meanings. The automobile driver learns the symbols for a railroad crossing, a curved road, and other hazards and restrictions. Symbols are widely used in advertising—remember the roaring lion used symbolically by Metro-Goldwyn-Mayer to suggest that their motion pictures surpassed all others, just as the king of beasts surpasses the other animals of the forest.

Symbols are used in religions, in paintings and sculpture, in legends and folklore, telling us something about a higher, more universal truth than is apparent in the world of objects. Thus they illuminate our understanding and enlarge our consciousness.

The fascinating Tarot symbols can open up a new world of ideas; as we study, we begin to see them as a sort of shorthand which, when we can read it, leads to realms of discovery. We find these symbols in ancient and modern art, in myth, fairy tale, and history. They give us revealing glimpses of the mystic traditions of the ancient world and open the way to the heights of spiritual and occult understanding.

And the Tarot abounds in the symbolism of Astrology and Numerology, as we shall see when we study the hidden meanings of the seventy-eight cards.

The
Minor Arcana

Lesson 2

GENERAL OBSERVATIONS

General Observations: As we have said, the Minor Arcana (forerunners of our own playing cards) are divided into four suits: Wands, Cups, Swords, and Pentacles. The number of suits, four, has symbolical significance. In ancient times it was thought that the world and everything in it was composed of a combination of just four elements: Air, Earth, Fire, and Water. The sacred name of Jehovah, creator of all things, was represented by the four letters IHVH, and was associated with the four elements with which He worked.

Later, these elements also were believed to have a relationship to the four stationary or fixed signs of the Zodiac—Taurus, Leo, Scorpio, and Aquarius—and they in turn correspond to the bull, the lion, the eagle, and the angel mentioned in the Bible (Ezekiel 1:10, Revelation 4:7), which decorate the four corners of two of the Major Arcana—the Wheel of Fortune and the World. There are four seasons also, and four points of the compass.

Some of the symbolism was derived from old Germanic mythology, where certain real or imaginary creatures were associated with the elements. The salamander, supposed to be unscathed by fire, was chosen to represent Fire; the undine, a female water sprite, was associated with Water; the sylph, an elemental of the air, with Air; and a little gnome, with Earth.

WANDS: Fire, Lion, South, Salamander
CUPS: Water, Water-Carrier, West, Undine

SWORDS: Air, Eagle, North, Sylph
PENTACLES: Earth, Bull, East, Gnome

The Meanings of the Suits in Divination:

WANDS: Energy, growth, enterprise, animation, glory.

The wands are of green wood that retains a few live twigs, signifying growth. They are sometimes used as a club in fighting or as a staff to carry a victor's crown. Their position in relation to the other cards in a layout will determine whether this energy will be constructive or destructive. Wands are associated with the world of ideas and with creation and agriculture. The suit of clubs used in modern playing cards was derived from the Wands.

CUPS: Love, happiness, the emotions, fertility, beauty.

Cups, which appear in all the cards of this suit, are associated with water, a symbol of the subconscious mind and the instincts, as opposed to the conscious mind and reason. The modern suit of hearts is derived from the Cups.

SWORDS: Aggression, force, ambition, courage, strife, misfortune.

Many cards of this suit depict fighting or people who are bowed down with misfortune. Swords represent the world of action, both constructive and destructive. They correspond to the spades in the modern deck.

PENTACLES: Money, industry, material gain.

Except for the Five of Pentacles, these cards all depict people either working with or enjoying the fruits of labor. The coinlike disks are pentacles, here inscribed with pentagrams—five-pointed stars that are time-honored symbols of Man. In ancient days, people wore pentacles decorated with magic symbols as a protection from the evils of life.

The Symbology of Numbers: Understanding the symbology of numbers as they are found in the Minor Arcana can be of great help in learning the meanings of the cards. In order to emphasize this relationship I have grouped the cards in a numerical arrangement.

The aces of the four suits are grouped together, followed by the twos, threes, and so on. In this way the meanings of the cards are shown as they relate to both their numbers and their suits. For example, the Number Five is thought of as an unfavorable number, and the fives of all the suits are considered "unhappy" cards; but their negative aspects are modified by the overall meaning of each specific suit and the place that the particular five occupies in the final layout.

In symbolism, numbers mean not only quantities, as in mathematics, but also ideas, each with its own particular meaning and force. All numbers are derived from Number One, the first point of expression from the nonmanifest into the manifest. The farther a number is from One, the more deeply it is involved in matter. Number One can be said to be the active principle that, when broken into fragments, gives rise to the multiplicity.

In order to accustom yourself to handling the cards, I suggest that you lay out the four aces in a row on the table. Below them, arrange the twos and threes before you turn the page and begin to study their meanings.

Lesson 3

THE ACES, TWOS, AND THREES

The Aces: The Number One, or Ace, is Alpha, the beginning of all things, the number of creative power and individuality. It is the primary number from which all others are evolved, and is equated with the one God and the oneness of Man.

The Twos: One engenders two, and two creates three. Now, we have in the Number Two pairs of opposites—positive and negative, day and night, male and female, spirit and form. This duality is expressed in the cards below as a balance of forces; it indicates creativity not yet fulfilled.

The Threes: Three is the number of growth and expression, the trinity of life. In three, we have man, woman, and then the child; seed, earth, and then the plant. Ideas are worked out in the mind, and then comes the material result. Number One contains the idea; Number Two, the pair who can carry out the idea; and in Number Three we have the fruits of the partnership or mating. Three also represents man's triune nature—spirit, mind, and body.

ACE of WANDS.

There is something serene and yet strong about the hand that emerges from the clouds offering a flowering wand. There are eight leaves floating down (eight is the number denoting material and spiritual progress and balance). The castle on the hill stands like a promise of what the future may hold.

Interpretation: A creative beginning. A new business venture or perhaps a profitable journey. The card can also be read as suggesting an inheritance, a new career, or a birth in the family.

Reversed: Selfishness may spoil the venture; the new enterprise will have setbacks; a journey may be put off; there may be a lack of determination to see a project through.

ACE ᲘᲘ CUPS.

Five streams of water, symbols of the five senses, spring from the cup and fall into a pond; water lilies float on it. A dove of the spirit descends holding a wafer in its mouth. The drops of water falling from the cup suggest the Hebrew letter Yod, meaning the descent of the Life-force from above. The falling leaves in the Ace of Wands and the drops of dew in Key 18, the Moon, have the same implication.

Interpretation: The beginning of all good things, whether it be love, joy, beauty, or health. A new breakthrough in spiritual understanding.

Reversed: Hesitancy to accept the things of the heart. Perhaps a selfish grasping at love or a too-materialistic viewpoint that puts the joys of life to flight. Egotism.

Though the sword is two-edged and can cut both ways, its point is encircled by a crown from which hangs the olive branch of peace and the palm of victory. Six Yods hover above the handle—the Number Six meaning harmony and knowledge.

Interpretation: Beginning of a conquest or victory. The birth of a child who could be a valiant leader. The ability to both love and hate with ardor. The Seeker might become a champion in some field of endeavor.

Reversed: The two-edged sword can have a destructive effect as well as a constructive one. It also can separate the good from the bad. *Beware* of trying to use too much power to gain an end. The indication is that of meeting obstacles and tyranny.

Here, again, a hand comes out of the clouds, this time offering a pentacle. The garden below is well tended, and the lilies of spiritual thought grow from its soil. As pentacles indicate material gain and money, this card is a good one for a person interested in new ventures in finance.

Interpretation: Since an ace always signifies the beginning of a matter, here we have an indication of the beginning of prosperity or a business venture. There may also be an inheritance. There should also be a beginning here for the Seeker of happiness and pleasure in the good things of life.

Reversed: Caution—the love of wealth may turn to greed or miserliness. Great plans may come to naught. Comfortable material conditions may not be to the advantage of the Seeker.

Keeping in mind that the Wands signify enterprise, energy, and growth, we see a merchant or man of property looking out to sea, hoping his ships will come in fully laden. On the battlements of his castle is a design consisting of the white lilies of pure thought, balanced with the red roses of desire, indicating a well-balanced nature.

Interpretation: A person both kind and generous, who waits to see his plans bear fruit. An interest in the sciences may be indicated. Creative ability, courage, good things to come.

Reversed: A good beginning may not bear fruit; caution is advised against impatience. There is a possibility of domination by others.

This card is a good example of the balance of forces, with the man and woman pledging their troth. Cups are the cards of love and the emotions—hence the pair of young lovers. The serpents of good and evil are twined around a staff—a phallic emblem of life's positive and negative energies. Lions symbolically denote brute force and carnal desire, but in this case the lion has the wings of spirit, indicating a good balance between spiritual and earthly love.

Interpretation: The beginning of a new romance or a well-balanced friendship. Ideas generated between two partners. Harmony, cooperation, a well-balanced personality.

Reversed: Loss of balance in a relationship. A too-violent passion. Love turning to its opposite. A misunderstanding with someone the Seeker values highly.

Here we have the balance of two again, now influenced by the suit of Swords. The young woman seated on the bench is blindfolded indicating that she cannot see her way through the present situation. Behind her is the sea of her emotions, from which the jagged rocks of hard facts jut out. A treacherous new moon shines down upon her. The swords she raises are balanced for the present, but she is in a precarious situation.

Interpretation: There is a need for well-balanced emotions. A stalemate in one's affairs, indecision. Possible trouble ahead. A temporary truce in family quarrels. The Seeker has a well-developed sense of balance and rhythm, but is in need of direction.

Reversed: Release, movement in one's affairs, but sometimes in the wrong direction—for the rocks are still there. Caution against dealing with the unscrupulous.

Perhaps this young man is juggling two propositions, trying to decide which to accept. Behind him the sea of his emotions is rough; the ships of his ideas are having a hard time staying afloat. He seems rather lighthearted, however, as he gaily balances the pentacles.

Interpretation: The ability to handle several situations or business proposals at a time. The Seeker is able to maintain harmony in the midst of change. New projects may be difficult to launch. A helpful message can be expected.

Reversed: Here we find that the Seeker is having difficulty in handling his problems. He has too many irons in the fire. A discouraging message is likely to put a damper on his ideas. Plans may go awry.

Here we have the merchant shown in the Two of Wands; he can now see his ships returning to him from across the waters of his subconscious. His grasp on a wand is firm, for he has staked his claim and now can receive the results.

Interpretation: There will be cooperation in business affairs; trade and commerce will flourish. A good partnership brings success. Practical help may come from a successful person.

Reversed: There is a tendency to scatter one's energies. Mistakes may be made through carelessness. The wonderful business venture may be a disappointment. Caution against pride and arrogance.

Three young maidens hold high their cups, which contain "the wine of life." Fruitful garlands and vines lie at their feet. Perhaps they are offering a toast to love.

Interpretation: Good fortune in love; happy conclusion of an undertaking, perhaps in the arts. The Seeker may have unsuspected talents in music or painting. He is sensitive and sympathetic to others. There is hospitality—perhaps a party—in the offing.

Reversed: Pleasure turns to pain. Beware of gossip from an old friend. Talents and abilities lie hidden. Overindulgence in food and drink. Abundance may turn to want.

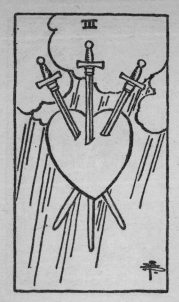

Rain and clouds in the background, and a heart pierced by three swords. In the Kabalah, the mother figure Binah (third Sephiroth*) is sometimes depicted as a heart pierced by swords. The fullness of expression of sorrow.

Interpretation: Stormy weather for the affections. A separation may be pending as the result of a quarrel. Lovers are separated by war or misfortune. Upheaval in the family. Possibility of civil war or political strife.

Reversed: Here the general meaning remains the same, but not so extreme. Disorder, confusion, loss. Later, when you are doing a reading, the cards near the Three of Swords will indicate the degree of sorrow that comes with loss.

* One of the ten globes of the Tree of Life in the Kabalah. See also Geburah under the Five of Wands.

A sculptor is carving in a church or monastery. He consults with a nun and a monk, who hold out a scroll to him. Compare this card with the Eight of Pentacles. These cards often come up in a reading for an artist or craftsman.

Interpretation: Skill and ability are rewarded. The master craftsman is approved and applauded. Congratulations may be due soon. Material gain, success through effort. This card may indicate that the Seeker is a member of the Masonic Order or some other guild or fraternity.

Reversed: Mediocrity in workmanship. The coveted contract is delayed. Preoccupation with money at the expense of good work. Commonplace ideals and ambitions.

Lesson 4

THE FOURS, FIVES, AND SIXES

The Fours: The number Four stands for the cube or square, equally divided. It is the number of reality, the material universe, logic, and reason. Through incarnation the divine image of man as a threefold being is brought to the material plane, forming a square. Man's divine destiny is to learn to express consciously, through his life on earth, the perfection that he already possesses in spirit.

The Fives: Five is the number of uncertainty. It carries no constant vibration; it may shift and change. It can indicate uncontrolled activity and swing to the depths of despair. It is symbolized by the five-pointed star, the pentagram. The fives in the Tarot pack signify more adversity than one generally finds in books on Numerology. We may get a hint of the meaning of five from the Tree of Life of the Kabalah, described extensively in my book, *A Complete Guide to the Tarot.*

The Sixes: The number of marriage, motherhood, and harmony, the Six stands for balance and equilibrium. Its solidity is represented by the six-sided cube. The six-pointed star, called the Seal of Solomon, is formed by superimposing two triangles, one with the point up (for the trinity of spirit), the other with the point down (for the trinity of earth). Six is primarily the number of the mind.

Garlands of flowers form a triumphal arch for the approaching people, who hold their bouquets high. Behind them is a bridge over a moat, which leads to a turreted castle. Here we have the four of solidity and the material universe mingled with the energy and growth characteristics of the Wands, and the result is bound to be a happy, productive card.

Interpretation: The beauty of the harvest home. Perfected work, prosperity, peace. Celebration after labor. Romance may end in marriage. Happy holidays to come.

Reversed: This is such a good card that even reversed it carries much the same message, but in lesser degree. Learn to appreciate the little things of life, the beauty of nature, peace and harmony among friends and family.

A young man, seated in contemplation, gazes at the three cups before him. The emotional nature of the suit of Cups is here turned inward, for he is offered another cup from the world of spirit—and he refuses them all. He may well represent the intellect as it ponders the material and spiritual, the worlds of action and thought.

Interpretation: A time for reevaluation. Dissatisfaction with material success; world-weariness. Emotions turned inward; kindness and understanding will come from others.

Reversed: New relationships now possible. There is a desire for work and accomplishment, new goals, new ambitions. There will be a turning to the world of action.

The effigy of a knight reposes upon his tomb, his hands in an attitude of prayer. Three swords hang over him; the fourth is fastened to the side of his tomb. The Number Four has sometimes been called the number of defeat, poverty, and misery. Its basic meaning is the reality of the material universe. Perhaps this knight has been shorn of his glory through the forces of logic and reason.

Interpretation: Time of repose; rest after war and strife. THIS IS NOT A CARD OF DEATH. For the Seeker it could mean a time of retreat, a sense of banishment or temporary exile. Convalescence after illness. There will soon be a change back to the active life.

Reversed: Renewed activity. Caution to use discretion in all one's dealings. May indicate social unrest, labor strikes.

A miser, who toiled in the city behind him, now hangs on tightly to the gold for which he has labored. This card expresses the solidity and strength of purpose of the Number Four, coupled with the money and success aspects of the Pentacles.

Interpretation: Love of earthly power and money; the give-and-take of life is lacking here, and there are indications of a miserly, ungenerous character. A gift or inheritance may arrive shortly.

Reversed: Chance of loss of some earthly possessions. In business there will be obstacles, delay, and opposition. A spendthrift, too free with his money.

Five young men are brandishing huge staves as if in combat. Are they in earnest? Wands are identified with enterprise and glory, so perhaps these youths are seeking the challenge of battle.

Interpretation: Competition in the Seeker's field of activity is strong. Possibility of a lawsuit, a quarrel with a neighbor. Obstacles. Courage and the willingness to fight for one's right may change things for the better.

Reversed: Here we have the direct opposite of strife— harmony in one's affairs, new opportunities. Love of exercise and games. Generosity, which may run to prodigality. On the Tree of Life, No. 5, Geburah, represents the breaking-down force of nature, which is as necessary as the building-up force.

The wine of life has been spilled on the ground, and a man in a black cloak looks on in despair. Behind him remain two full cups, but he does not heed them. In the distance flows the stream of the subconscious, and beyond that a bridge leads to a remote castle. Here we have the emotions of the Cups, together with the Number Five, which betokens despair and agony over some great loss.

Interpretation: Sorrow. Loss of a loved one. A marriage seems on the point of breaking up. The wine of life has been bitter, and the Seeker refuses to turn and see the cups behind him still full of promise. Disillusionment, vain regret—but with something still remaining.

Reversed: Return of hope, new alliances formed, return of an old friend or loved one. Courage is summoned up to overcome difficulties.

Storm clouds fill the sky as a rogue looks scornfully back at the adversaries whose swords he has captured. The Seeker may be either the conquered or the conqueror, depending on what the cards next to this one indicate in the spread.

Interpretation: Failure, defeat, degradation, or conquest by unfair means over others. Cowardliness, cruelty, malice. Theft that could be an empty victory.

Reversed: There is still a chance of loss or defeat, but in lesser degree. An empty victory. There will be unfairness and slyness in dealings with others.

Two wayfarers in a snowstorm pass under a lighted church window. One is lame, the other destitute. Here we see the reverse of the usual good fortune betokened by the Pentacles. This message may be a deeper one than just lack of money and health, for these two may have failed to grasp the inner spiritual light.

Interpretation: Destitution, loneliness, loss of home and possessions. Lovers unable to find a meeting place. Possibility of poor health, which should be watched. Spiritual impoverishment leads to despair. Dark night of the soul.

Reversed: A lesson in charity is to be learned. New employment, but this may not be permanent. Revived courage. A new interest in spiritual matters.

The man on horseback is a conqueror, for he wears the laurel wreath of victory and carries another wreath on his staff. The common people walk beside him in admiration. Here are combined the energy and enterprise of the Wands with mental qualities of leadership.

Interpretation: Good news. Victory will be achieved; success will be attained through labor. Advancement will come in the arts and sciences, and an increasing harmony in relationships. Friends are helpful. Possible journey as a leader.

Reversed: Rewards are delayed; the trip is postponed. Bad news may come of another's victory. The winner may be insolent. Pride in riches and success.

A boy is offering a little girl a cup filled with flowers. Nearby five more cups hold flowers. They stand on a quaint old village green; the thatched cottage behind them conveys thoughts of home and childhood memories.

Interpretation: Meeting with a childhood acquaintance who has a gift for the Seeker. Happiness and enjoyment that come from the past. Pleasant memories. Or the meaning may be a new friendship or a gift from an admirer. New surroundings and opportunities. Possibility of an inheritance.

Reversed: Clinging to outworn morals and manners. Living in the past instead of the present. Outworn friendships should be discarded. Disappointment over an inheritance that may not be as large as the Seeker had hoped.

Here we have an interesting combination of the harmony
of the Number Six with Swords, which often betoken
strife and misfortune. A ferryman carries a sorrowing
woman and child across the water to the farther shore.
Note that the water on the right side of the boat is rough
and on the left, calm.

Interpretation: Journey by water. Passage away from
difficulties and sorrow. Harmony will again prevail. The
Seeker may send someone else to represent him in an
important meeting. The journey may be done in consciousness that will raise the Seeker out of his difficulties to a
more understanding frame of mind.

Reversed: No immediate way out of present difficulties. A
planned journey will be postponed. A journey into a
higher consciousness is advisable.

The meaning of this card is alms with justice. We see a merchant weighing out gold in a scale, so that he can distribute it with balanced judgment.

Interpretation: Present prosperity shared with others. The Seeker will receive what is rightfully his. Philanthropy, charity, gifts. The bread thrown upon the waters of life will come back threefold.

Reversed: Gifts given, but as a bribe. Unfairness in business or in the distribution of an estate. Present prosperity threatened; jealousy, miserliness.

Lesson 5

THE SEVENS, EIGHTS, NINES, AND TENS

The Sevens: Seven is a number of great significance that carries profound undertones. This number denotes wisdom, perfection, completeness; it is the number of the mystic, and relates to the soul development of the individual; also to the completed cycle of physical labors. "God rested on the seventh day ... And God blessed the seventh day and sanctified it." There are seven major planets, seven notes in the scale, seven days in the week, seven virtues, seven vices, and seven deadly sins.

The Eights: Eight is the number of justice, judgment, material progress, and health. It is a symbol of regeneration and the balance of opposing forces. Sometimes cited as the number of death and destruction, it really betokens death of the old, the evil, the wrong, to make way for the new, the pure, the just. The wise man dies a little every day in shedding old concepts, old habits, and old methods of thinking and living.

The Nines: In this number, all the forces of the other numbers are summed up. It is symbolical of attainment on the three planes of being: physical, mental, and spiritual. Nine is commanded to be perfect in Ten, which is the One of beginning placed beside the Zero of Spirit, after which man begins on a higher level.

The Tens: The meaning of Ten is perfection through completion. From unity (One) evolves duality (Two), producing the trinity (three) and leading to the square (Four), completing the cycle in Ten and resolving to unity again. The Ten in the suits of the Minor Arcana is the ultimate quintessence of each suit. The "good" suits, Cups and Pentacles, show the height of bliss; the "bad" suits, Wands and Swords, show the depths of tribulation—the ultimate, the completed force whether for good or evil.

In the time of Queen Elizabeth I, men fought with quarter staves, just as the youth is doing here. Six enemies are attacking from below. One of the attributes of seven is deep purpose and valor, both of which are displayed here.

Interpretation: The ability to hold one's own against adversaries. There will be stiff competition in business. If this card comes up in the Seeker's past, he has already won the fight; if in the future, this is something he may have to face soon. Victory depends on energy, courage.

Reversed: The threat will pass you by. Don't let others take advantage of you. Caution against indecision. Patience in the face of wrangling and threats.

Fantastic visions rise out of the seven cups in the clouds before this man. He does not know which to choose—the castle, the jewels, the wreath of victory with the skull below it, the red dragon of temptation, or the serpent of jealousy. The head with curling hair might be a woman— or his ideal of himself. In the center is a draped figure, his own divinity waiting to be uncovered.

Interpretation: An imagination that has been working overtime. Dissipated forces; the inability to choose one's direction in life. Selfish indulgence in dreams instead of action. Illusory success.

Reversed: Good use of determination and will. A definite project will be selected. Any small success must be followed up.

A man is seen escaping with a bundle of swords he has stolen from the military encampment below. Two swords remain impaled in the ground.

Interpretation: An unwise attempt to take what is not one's own. Unreliability, betrayal of confidence; insolence and spying. A plan that may fail. Flight from the consequences of a dishonorable act.

Reversed: The Seeker brings more to situations than is required. Good advice and counsel are given. A thief returns what he has stolen.

A young farmer leans on his hoe and intently studies the vine he is cultivating. The seven days of labor are finished, but he hesitates before accepting the harvest.

Interpretation: Growth through effort and hard work. Pause during development of an enterprise concerning money, a loan, an exchange, or sale. What has been planted may not mature. The artist reevaluates his work.

Reversed: Little gain after much work. Impatience. Anxiety about a loan or business deal. Unprofitable investments.

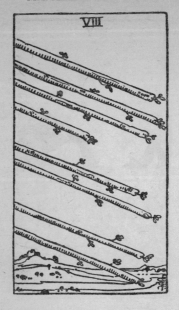

A flight of wands across the countryside. They seem to have come to rest, their energy spent.

Interpretation: Approach to a goal. New ideas will receive swift action. Journey by air. Arrows of love find their mark. Love of open air, gardens, meadows, field sports.

Reversed: Arrows of jealousy and violence. Quarrels, domestic disputes. The awaited message does not arrive. The force of courage and boldness applied too suddenly.

A man with a staff walks away from all that he previously held dear. The eight cups stacked so neatly show his previous concern and care. Now he turns his back on them and heads toward the barren mountains. Perhaps he is seeking something higher than material success and pleasures. The moon, in both its full and its waning quarter, looks on.

Interpretation: Rejection of the material life; abandonment of one's present mode of life. Disappointment in love. Misery and repining without cause, for the cups are still full. Desire to leave material success for something higher.

Reversed: Search for pleasure; interest in success, joy, feasting. A new love interest appears on the horizon. The spiritual aspects of life are left for the more unworldly.

A maiden stands bound and blindfolded in a marshy place. Swords form a barrier around her. A castle appears on a rocky promontory on the horizon.

Interpretation: The Seeker is fearful of moving out of a situation of bondage. Restricted action through indecision. Those around him hold him too tightly. Censure. Temporary illness has left the Seeker too weak to fight for his rights. Someone he knows is a prisoner—either military or civil.

Reversed: Relaxation from fear. New beginnings now possible. Freedom from restrictions. The person in prison will soon be released.

The sculptor's apprentice is carving out some pentacles. Compare this card with the Three of Pentacles, in which the sculptor has become a mature artist. This card often comes up in the layout of one who is studying the arts.

Interpretation: Learning a trade or profession. Employment or commission to come. Skill in material affairs, handiwork, and the arts—but only in the apprenticeship stage. Gain of money in small sums.

Reversed: Wrong use of skills. Intrigue and sharp dealing. Dislike of hard work, false vanity, voided ambition. Overcarefulness in small things at the expense of more important matters.

A man stands ready to defend his territory. From the bandage on his head it is evident he has fought before, and he is ready to fight again for what is right. The Five, Seven, and Nine of Wands all show men in a fighting mood.

Interpretation: Preparedness. Eventual victory, but more fighting must be done. If attacked, the person involved will defend himself stoutly. Good health. Strength in reserve. A tendency to obstinacy.

Reversed: Unpreparedness. Refusal to fight for what is thought right. Weakness of character; ill health. Bending under adversity.

This is the wish card, a key card on which the results of the Seeker's question can depend. A substantial, well-fed man sits with his arms crossed in satisfaction. His nine cups on the arched shelf behind him seem to guarantee his future well-being.

Interpretation: Material success, assured future. Physical well-being. A love of sensual pleasures. The Seeker will get his wish.

Reversed: Lack of material goods and money; overindulgence in food and drink. There may be some deprivation and illness, but not of a lasting nature. The Seeker's wish will not be fulfilled.

A sleepless woman sits on her couch, her head in her hands in apparent despair. Nine swords hang over her. Her coverlet is decorated with zodiacal signs, and the panel under her couch appears to bear a picture of two swordsmen—one fallen at the thrust of the other. In the Two, Four, Eight, Nine, and Ten of Swords, a person is immobilized by misfortune or disaster.

Interpretation: Suffering, desolation, doubt, suspicion. May mean the illness, injury, or death of a loved one. Cruelty, pitilessness, loss, misery, lying dishonesty, slander.

Reversed: Time brings healing. Patience, unselfishness, faithfulness are urged. Good news of a loved one. Tomorrow is another day.

A mature, well-dressed woman stands alone in her vineyard. The falcon on her gloved hand is suggestive of well-controlled thoughts. Her manor house can be seen in the background. This card often appears in the layout of a woman who is either widowed or single, and who has sufficient of the world's goods to enjoy the good life—but she is alone.

Interpretation: Material well-being. Solitary enjoyment of the good things of life. Wisdom where one's own interests lie. A person with a green thumb who has a great love for her garden and home. Caution to be prudent. Possibility of an inheritance.

Reversed: Possible loss, perhaps of a friendship or a home. Danger from thieves. Beware of legal entanglements. Move with caution.

The man depicted is carrying a heavy burden consisting of ten flowering wands. The burden seems almost more than he can manage, yet he plods along to the city.

Interpretation: One who is carrying an oppressive load, either mentally or physically. His heart is tried by pain. Ruin of all plans and projects. Complete disruption and failure.

Reversed: Strength and energy applied to selfish ends. A desire to ruin the happiness of others. A clever, eloquent person who knows how to shift burdens from himself to others.

This is the ultimate of what the Cups can bring in the way of love and happiness. The young couple stretch forth their arms in gratitude toward the rainbow of promise; their children dance for joy. Their modest home is in the background. Compare this card with the Ten of Pentacles, where great wealth also enters the picture.

Interpretation: Happy family life. True friendships. Here is lasting happiness inspired from above, instead of the sensual satisfaction seen in the Nine of Cups.

Reversed: A family quarrel, loss of friendships, chance of betrayal. Some damage may be done to the home. Youngsters turn against their parents. Wantonness, waste, debauchery.

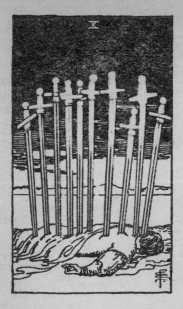

A man pierced by ten swords lies in a desolate waste. In the Four, Six, Eight, and Nine of this suit, the swords merely surround the people; in this card they actually pierce the man. They symbolize the ultimate of what strife, hatred, and aggression can do.

Interpretation: Sudden misfortune; ruin of plans. Defeat in war; a legal battle lost. Failure, pain, tears. BUT NOT A CARD OF DEATH. In giving a Tarot reading, death is never predicted or even hinted at.

Reversed: Overthrow of evil forces. Courage to rise again. Some success and profit. Enjoyment of better health. In spiritual matters, the Seeker now may turn to higher powers for help.

The head of the clan, a grandfather in robes of mystic design, is seated in the foreground surrounded by his family and dogs. His castle stands behind the archway on which is inscribed his coat of arms. The fullness of established trade, industry, family tradition, and great financial stability.

Interpretation: Family matters stabilized. Gain in wealth and prestige. Property is acquired; financial affairs prosper. Inheritance is more than was expected.

Reversed: Chance of family misfortune or loss of honor. Caution against getting involved in a project that may prove to be a poor risk. A problem arises concerning a will or pension. Dullness of mind and slothfulness.

Lesson 6

THE COURT CARDS

Each of the four suits of the Minor Arcana consists of not only numbered cards but also court cards. These are the King, Queen, Knight, and Page. In very old Tarot decks, I understand there was no Queen, her place being taken by the Knight. The change to include a Queen seems to have been made when cards became the favorite recreation of western European court circles. In some decks, the positions of the King and the Knight were reversed, since it was thought that the more important figure must be the one on horseback. Thus, the Queen had the Knight for her consort and the King was their son. But these past inconsistencies need not bother us now, for in all Tarot decks available at the present time, the suits contain all four members of the court.

The cards from ace to ten indicate events, and the court cards indicate the people to whom these events happen. To make a reading more personal, a court card is selected from the pack to represent the Seeker. It is called a Significator.

Kings represent men Knights represent young men

Queens represent women Pages represent both boys and girls

How to Select a Court Card for the Seeker

For people with blond hair and blue eyes—WANDS
For people with light brown hair and hazel eyes—CUPS

For people with brown hair and brown eyes—SWORDS
For people with black hair and black eyes—PENTACLES

Here I am reminded of a letter I got from a young girl
who wrote frantically to ask what to do about people with
red hair and green eyes—obviously herself. Well, it is a
problem if you are working with a person who does not fit
exactly into any of the above descriptions. The man or
woman Seeker may have gray hair, which has been dyed,
or even a wig. Personally, I do not believe that it makes a
crucial difference. If an older man is obviously in industry,
I suggest you choose the King of Pentacles in spite of the
Seeker's coloring. If you are reading for a woman, she
might like to have you read the characteristics of the four
Queens and let her decide which one she resembles most
closely. Or you might find a more suitable card in the
Major Arcana—for example, a Hierophant for a minister;
the Chariot for a soldier; and the Empress for an "earth
mother" type.

Now draw out the sixteen court cards from the pack
and line them up on your table, laying the Pages in a row,
then the Knights, and so forth—starting with the Wands
on your left and remembering that the Wands stand for
blond, blue-eyed people; the Cups for light brown; the
Swords for dark brown and the Pentacles for black hair.
You will notice that though the court cards are supposed
to represent people, they can also indicate qualities of
character and even events.

A. E. Waite, in his book *The Pictorial Key to the Tarot*
(this is the book that originally used the Waite Tarot
designs), suggests that the Major Arcana belongs to the
divine dealings of philosophy, but that the Minor Arcana
is primarily useful in divination. We feel there is much
philosophical content in the Minor Arcana; these cards
can be profitably studied for the light they shed on our
lives.

PAGE of WANDS.

The Book *T* of the Hermetic Order of the Golden Dawn, founded in England in 1886, calls the Page of Wands the Princess of the Shining Flame and the Rose of the Palace of Fire. Of the four elements that comprise the world— Fire, Water, Air, and Earth—the Wands correspond with the element Fire.

The figure in this card is holding a wand and seems about to deliver a message. CHOOSE THIS CARD FOR A BOY OR GIRL WITH BLOND HAIR AND BLUE EYES.

Interpretation: Brilliance, courage, beauty. A person sudden in anger or love. He has great enthusiasm and a dynamic personality. He might be a messenger or a postman, "the bearer of tidings."

Reversed: Superficial, theatrical, unstable. If the Seeker is a woman, the young man involved may break her heart. There may be bad news.

PAGE of CUPS.

The suit of Cups is symbolic of the subconscious mind and the emotions, which are often represented by water. Behind this youth or maiden are rolling waves. The page holds a cup from which appears a fish—a symbol of an idea in the imagination. (This figure is sometimes called the Princess of the Waters and Lotus of the Palace of Floods.) CHOOSE THIS CARD FOR A BOY OR GIRL WITH LIGHT BROWN HAIR AND HAZEL EYES.

Interpretation: Gentleness, sweetness, kindness. Someone who is interested in poetry and the arts; dreamy at times yet courageous when courage is needed. News, perhaps the birth of a child.

Reversed: Selfishness and love of luxury. Little desire to create, not much imagination.

PAGE of SWORDS.

Swords correspond to the element Air. To show this, there are birds in the sky of all Swords court cards. Birds also stand for the processes of activation. The Swords, representing strife or aggression, carry out the latter meaning. There are also storm clouds in the sky. The ground under the youth's feet is rough and uneven. He grasps his sword with both hands as if on the alert. (This card is called the Princess of the Rushing Winds, Lotus of the Palace.) CHOOSE THIS CARD FOR A BOY OR GIRL WITH BROWN HAIR AND EYES.

Interpretation: The qualities of grace and dexterity, diplomacy and understanding. Certain types of spying. An upsetting message.

Reversed: A tendency to frivolity and cunning. An impostor is likely to be exposed. Possibility of ill health. Be prepared for the unexpected.

1 Magician
2 Ten Pent
3 9 cups
4 8 cup Reverse
5 Page Pent
6 9 Pent
7 Ace Sword Revers
8 High Priestess R
9 The Hanged man R
10 8 of Swords

1 F,P   RE
2 3 P
3 KN W
4 ACE cup
5 Fi W
6 TEN Cup
7 Fi cup
8 Seven cup
9 Enperor
10 Justice

KING PEN

FOUR SW
R

PAGE
ROD

KN S   7 SW

TEN RODs - ROD

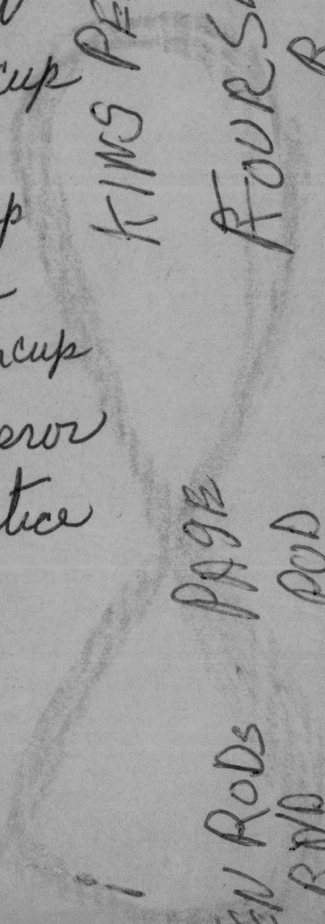

As married. The
One whom God
has chosen for
me to love and be
loved by

A youth stands in a field dotted with flowers and looks intently at the pentacle that seems almost to float in the air. Pentacles indicate money and earthly possessions; this page is careful and diligent. There may be good news. (This card is called Princess of the Echoing Hills, Rose of the Palace of Earth.) CHOOSE THIS CARD FOR A BOY OR GIRL WITH BLACK HAIR AND EYES.

Interpretation: A persevering scholar. Someone who is generous, kind, and careful, with respect for learning, new ideas, and opinions.

Reversed: Wastefulness, love of luxury. Rebelliousness. Surrounded by people with ideas in opposition to his own. Unfavorable news.

A young knight in armor comes galloping across the plains; three pyramids in the distance suggest the threefold principle of creation. Over his armor he wears a garment covered with salamanders—as do the Page and the King of Wands. (Since the salamander is the symbol of Fire, he is the Lord of the Flame and Lightning, King of the Spirit of Fire.) CHOOSE THIS CARD FOR A LIGHT-COMPLEXIONED YOUNG MAN.

Interpretation: A sudden and impetuous nature. The Seeker can be a generous friend or lover, but he has the capacity to create conflict and rivalry. He is hasty in all that he does. Perhaps there will be a journey or change of residence. The coming or going of a matter of much concern to the Seeker.

Reversed: Discord. Work interrupted. The friend or lover becomes jealous, even brutal. Narrow-mindedness, suspicion. Journey delayed.

KNIGHT of CUPS.

A handsome young man holds a cup in his hand as he rides over the green, peaceful countryside. He wears a winged helmet, sign of the imagination. (He is the Lord of the Waves and the Waters, King of the Hosts of the Sea.) CHOOSE THIS CARD FOR A YOUNG MAN WITH LIGHT BROWN HAIR AND HAZEL EYES.

Interpretation: A young man of high intelligence. A romantic dreamer. If the Seeker is a woman, she may be falling in love with such a young man. He is skilled in the arts, a good dancer or musician. The coming or going of a matter involving the emotions.

Reversed: Beware of trickery or fraud. Sensuality, idleness. He is often untruthful; his imagination runs away with him.

KNIGHT of SWORDS.

The symbolism is well worked out in this card with the sky full of storm clouds; a few birds fly in the wind that bends the cypress trees (symbols of sorrow). The rider charges forward as if to battle; birds and butterflies decorate the horse's harness. (This knight is called Lord of the Winds and the Breezes. King of the Spirits of Air.) CHOOSE THIS CARD FOR A YOUNG MAN WITH BROWN HAIR AND EYES.

Interpretation: One who is about to rush headlong into the life of the Seeker. A strong man, brave but domineering. He has great courage, is skillful and clever. May also mean the unexpected coming or going of a matter of great concern to the Seeker.

Reversed: Tyranny over the helpless, be it man or animal. Always ready to start a fight. A troublemaker and one who is crafty and secretive about his plans.

KNIGHT of PENTACLES

This knight rides a heavily caparisoned horse through a freshly plowed field. He wears a green branch in his helmet, and another decorates the front of his horse's bridle. He looks placidly at the pentacle he holds in front of him. (He is the Lord of the Wild and Fertile Land, King of the Spirits of Earth.) CHOOSE THIS CARD FOR A YOUNG MAN WITH BLACK HAIR AND EYES.

Interpretation: A methodical young man, thoroughly trustworthy but unimaginative. His outlook is heavy, dull, and material. Laborious and patient in material matters, he can accept responsibility. He is kind to animals and loves nature. The coming or going of a matter concerning money or land.

Reversed: Irresponsibility, impatience. He can be timid, careless, and even grasping. Money affairs seem to be at a standstill.

A stately queen sits on her throne, surrounded by symbols of the growth and energy of the Wands. In her left hand is a sunflower, showing she has control over nature. Lions, a symbol of Fire, form the arms of her throne; behind her is a panel of lions and sunflowers. The three pyramids of Nature rise in the background. Before her sits a black cat, the sinister aspect of Venus. (She is Queen of the Thrones of Flame.) CHOOSE THIS CARD FOR A BLONDE WITH BLUE EYES.

Interpretation: A woman who usually lives in the country and is fond of nature and of home. She has the power of attraction and command, but is well liked and honorable, sound in her judgments. If the card does not represent a woman, it represents the qualities mentioned.

Reversed: She may still be virtuous, but she is strict to a fault and domineering. A jealous and revengeful nature that can turn against others quickly. Deceit and infidelity are suggested.

From her throne a very beautiful woman, the crowned queen, gazes dreamily into the cup of her imagination, the handles of which are shaped like angels; the cup itself is closed, signifying that her thoughts are in the realm of the unconscious. (Queen of the Thrones of the Waters.) CHOOSE THIS CARD FOR A WOMAN WITH LIGHT BROWN HAIR AND HAZEL EYES.

Interpretation: A woman who has more feeling and imagination than common sense. She is, however, a good wife and loving mother. She is poetic, dreamy; kind but not often willing to give too much help to her friends. Happiness, pleasure of a gentle, good-natured sort.

Reversed: Her imagination runs away with her. A good woman in many ways, but perverse. She may mean well, but is not to be relied upon. Pleasure and happiness turn bitter.

A queen seated on a high throne looks out into a clouded sky. She rests the hilt of her sword on the arm of her throne, and holds out her left hand as if to beckon her subjects. Her crown and the base of her throne are decorated with butterflies and a sylph. A bird hovers above, and cypress trees appear in the background. (She is the Queen of the Thrones of the Air.) CHOOSE THIS CARD FOR A WOMAN WITH BROWN HAIR AND EYES.

Interpretation: A woman who is intensely perceptive, quick and confident in all she does. She may represent a widow or one who has no child or has lost one. A woman of strong character, she can bear her sorrow. The card can also mean that the sword of spirit penetrates matter and informs it.

Reversed: Her keen observations may lead her to be cruel to others. Sometimes she is both sly and deceitful. Narrowmindedness and a tendency to gossip.

QUEEN of PENTACLES

A dark, powerful woman, a Queen of Fertility, sits enthroned amidst the symbols of plenty. A bower of roses is above her; a cupid and ripe fruit decorate the back of her throne, and the head of a goat forms part of its arm. The scene is in the midst of green fertile fields; the rabbit of fertility rests in the grass at her feet. (She is the Queen of the Thrones of Earth.) CHOOSE THIS CARD FOR A WOMAN WITH BLACK HAIR AND EYES.

Interpretation: An intelligent and thoughtful woman who can create in numerous ways, in business as well as with children and gardens. She uses her talents well, is rich and charitable. At times she is melancholy and moody.

Reversed: Too much dependence on others. Duties neglected. Fear of failure. A mistrustful and suspicious nature. Not much creative ability. Changeable.

KING of WANDS

Lions and salamanders, symbols of Fire, are on the pillar behind the king. Salamanders also adorn his robe, and at his feet a live salamander looks on. Beneath his crown he wears the cap of maintenance, symbolizing authority. (He is the Prince of the Chariot of Fire.) CHOOSE THIS CARD FOR A MAN WITH BLUE OR HAZEL EYES AND BLOND HAIR.

Interpretation: A country gentleman, usually married and the father of a family. He is handsome and passionate; can be generous and noble yet strong and hasty. He is a good leader and agile in both mind and body.

Reversed: A severe, unyielding man, strict in his judgments. At times intolerant and prejudiced. Possibility that he will meet opposition or get into a quarrel.

KING of CUPS.

The king's throne rests upon a turbulent sea, from which a dolphin jumps; there is also a ship at anchor. The four court cards of the Cups all show water in some way— symbol of the subconscious, which in this instance seems troubled. Upon his breast the king wears a golden fish upon a chain. (Prince of the Chariot of the Waters.) CHOOSE THIS CARD FOR A MAN WITH LIGHT BROWN HAIR AND HAZEL EYES.

Interpretation: A man of business, law, or divinity; kind and considerate, and willing to take responsibility. He is interested in the arts and sciences. He covers his emotional nature with a calm exterior, and enjoys quiet power.

Reversed: A powerful man but likely to be double-dealing. A crafty, violent nature. There may be some scandal connected with him.

Behind the king are the storm clouds; also the cypress
trees and birds that have appeared in the other court
cards of Swords. He is a stern king and sits on his throne
as if in judgment. (He is the Prince of the Chariots of the
Winds.) CHOOSE THIS CARD FOR A MATURE MAN
WITH DARK HAIR AND EYES.

Interpretation: He is a judge, either military or civilian.
His is the power to command, the power of life and death.
He is firm in friendship or enmity, but suspicious and
overcautious. He may prove a wise counselor, full of
helpful ideas.

Reversed: His intentions are evil; he is obstinate and
malicious. Caution in getting embroiled in a ruinous
lawsuit. Judgments and decisions by those in authority do
not seem fair.

What richness surrounds this king, whose scepter shows his power and rule over all! His robe is embroidered with bunches of grapes and vine leaves; bulls' heads (for Taurus) are on the back and arms of his throne. His castle is in the background. (He is the Prince of the Chariot of Earth.) CHOOSE THIS CARD FOR A MAN WITH BLACK HAIR AND EYES.

Interpretation: A chief of industry, a banker, or owner of large estates. He is a reliable married man and probably has quite a few children. He has great financial gifts and is an accomplished mathematician. Solid and steady, he can be of help to the Seeker.

Reversed: He is too material; often appears stupid. He goes forward like an ox with his head to the ground. Though slow to anger, he can be dangerous when aroused. Perverse use of talents; a person easy to bribe.

Now put all your Minor Arcana cards away for the time being. Arrange the Major Arcana on the table before you in numerical order, so that you will become familiar not only with the illustrations in this book but also with the cards themselves.

The
Major Arcana

Lesson 7

GENERAL OBSERVATIONS

The Major Arcana consists of twenty-two very special cards that contain elements of philosophy embodying answers to the mysteries of creation, the origin of life, and the nature of Man. A. E. Waite, a foremost authority in the field, has said: "The true Tarot is symbolism. It speaks no other language and presents no other signs. ... On the highest plane it offers a key to the ancient mysteries." And, indeed, these symbols have profoundly impressed the members of the Western occult schools, who have been willing only in recent years to divulge the hidden meanings.

Whether the cards came originally from China or India is not known, but it is possible that the Gypsies brought them to Europe when they migrated there during the twelfth century, since we find the first reference to both the Gypsies and the Tarot in documents of this period. The Tarot cards were discovered—rather, rediscovered—by Court de Gébelin on a visit to Marseilles. Shortly thereafter he wrote about them in the eighth volume of his *Le Monde Primitif*, published between 1773 and 1782. No book of explanation had accompanied the cards Gébelin found, and the savants from that time to this have been trying to decipher their original meanings.

Some feel that the Major Arcana is older than the Minor Arcana, and that the *two* sections were put together at a later period. It is felt that the Minor Arcana may have originated for fortune-telling and games, whereas the Major Arcana was later adapted to divination. The answer is lost in antiquity, and we can only speculate on the accuracy of this theory.

Whoever the creators of the Major Arcana were, they must have been acquainted with the ancient Hebrew Kabalah. Not only does the number of Keys (twenty-two) correspond to the number of letters in the Hebrew alphabet, but many of the cards suggest symbolism derived from the Tree of Life that forms the basis of much of the kabalistic wisdom.

The meanings of the cards (Keys) of the Major Arcana are not clear at first sight without some instruction, for they do indeed contain the wisdom of the ages as it has appeared in legends, parables, and allegories, and in the scriptures of all religions. But in spite of their antiquity, the Tarot can easily be related to the problems and situations of our time.

The Fool, Key 0, has been placed before the remaining twenty-one cards, for he symbolizes you, me, everyone; and the cards that follow are the qualities we acquire and the life experiences we must go through if we are to have the type of spiritual realization shown in Key 21, where the lessons of life have been learned at last, and the mortal, central Self has reached its highest possible development on this plane.

Before the description of each card, I have included a paragraph called *in a reading*, which should be of great help to you when you have reached the point of doing practice readings. Often students seem to find making a cohesive story out of a spread a difficult thing to do. They know the symbolism of the cards, but not how to relate each card to those around it to make a complete story.

At any rate, it is well to remember that these twenty-two cards have a deep spiritual significance. I am sure you will feel their fascination as we study each of them in turn.

THE FIRST THIRD
OF THE MAJOR ARCANA

KEY 0

THE FOOL

The general meaning of this card is:
A CHOICE IS OFFERED

Interpretation: The Fool represents the beginning of all creativity and the desire to accomplish impossibly beautiful goals. Here are all the joys and possibilities of adventure. Each of us faces many choices in life. A fresh choice is before you—choose wisely.

Reversed: The choice is likely to be faulty and lead to thoughtless action. Fear may hold one back from accepting the new opportunity. Folly and indiscretion are suggested.

In a Reading: When this card appears in the future of the Seeker, it is read as a choice that will be offered him. If a card is near it, then the kind of person suggested by that card will be the one who offers the new opportunity.

If there are many Major Arcana in the spread, then the Seeker does not have much to say about it: the choice will be made by others. When the Fool is found in reverse, warn the Seeker that his choice is likely to be foolish and he should give it much thought. When it is found in the past, the Seeker has already made a choice of some importance, and the cards surrounding it will indicate whether the choice has been a good one. If he seems a timid sort, encourage the Seeker to think seriously about the new opportunity that lies before him.

Description: A youth looks out into the distance instead of at his feet, where the mountain crag falls away before him. He stands poised as if ready to take the next step, which will be down into the realm of matter. Seemingly in an expectant mood, he holds a white rose in his hand— symbol of spiritual desires. Over his shoulder he carries the Wand of Will, from which hangs a wallet containing the four elements Fire, Water, Air, and Earth, which he will use on his journey. At his feet a small dog prances to show that though the youth's ideals are lofty, the life of the senses will also accompany him on his journey.

THE MAGICIAN.

KEY 1

THE MAGICIAN

This is the card of:
CREATIVE POWER

Interpretation: He who can take the opportunities offered by this card will perhaps be a builder of new houses, an originator of inventions or new forms of art, or he may be creative in his home life. Here we have the ability to use the power from above and direct it into manifestation. Organizational skill is also suggested.

Reversed: The use of power for destructive ends. Ineptitude. A project fails. Plans are poorly constructed.

In a Reading: If this card covers that of the Seeker, you are reading for a most dynamic person. If you find this card in his future, you can predict he will have organizational ability and be very creative in his chosen field. If this card falls in his past, then he had these abilities and demonstrated them in relation to the question he has asked. The cards that follow will show if he has been successful. In reverse, however, this card may indicate he has used, or will use, his power for destructive ends, perhaps to "get even" with someone. Or it may indicate he has a weak will; in this case try to encourage him to be more forceful and creative.

Description: He stands in an attitude of power and command, holding his wand high over his head to receive from above that which he transmutes to earthly things as he points below in a gesture of creation. Above his head is the cosmic lemniscate, a figure 8 in a horizontal position—a symbol of eternal life and dominion.

On the table lie the four symbols of creation: the wand standing for Fire; the cup, for Water; the sword, for Air; and the pentacle, for Earth. He will use these elements in his creations. Below him the white lilies of pure abstract thought intertwine with the red roses of desire; more roses form a bower above him. About his waist is a snake devouring its tail, a well-known symbol of eternity.

The Magician represents the personal will in union with the Divine will, which gives him the power and the knowledge to create with the tools before him. The Number One, as explained in connection with the aces in the Minor Arcana, fits perfectly in this instance.

THE HIGH PRIESTESS

KEY 2

THE HIGH PRIESTESS

The meaning of this card:

HIDDEN INFLUENCES

Interpretation: Unrevealed future; the mystery of things hidden in the depths of consciousness. Spiritual enlightenment, inner illumination. A caution not to speak of that which should be kept secret. In a man's reading, this card represents the perfect woman all men dream of; in a woman's reading, it may indicate virtues in a friend or in herself.

Reversed: A selfish and ruthless woman. A life of indulgence and outward show. Conceit. Only surface knowledge. In a man's reading, this card means he must be careful not to be destroyed by a woman's selfishness.

In a Reading: This interesting card contains a number of symbols, but the main meanings concern the hidden matters suggested by the moon. In a reading for an artist, it means that he gets many of his ideas through intuition. In a man's reading, the High Priestess suggests that he will meet an understanding woman just right for him. If the card is in the past, he has already met her, and the next few cards show whether he has recognized this treasure or passed her by. In reverse, the card indicates that a conceited, selfish woman is mixed up in the question asked. If the High Priestess is in a woman's cards, it shows her own nature and how she will handle the working out of her question.

Description: The High Priestess has the crescent moon at her feet and wears a crown that shows a full moon with crescent moons on either side. She is the virgin daughter of the moon and corresponds to all the virgin goddesses of the ancient world and to the Virgin Mary. On her lap is a scroll of the Tora (Divine Law), and on her breast a solar cross with arms of equal length; the upright arm is the male or positive force, and the horizontal is the female or negative. The primal unit is now divided into two, and their eternal propensity to reunite results in creation, thus forming the trinity of father, mother, and son.

Behind her are the two pillars of Solomon's Temple— Boaz the black, to indicate the negative Life-force, and Jachin, the positive. The veil between them, a symbol of virginity, is embroidered with palms (male) and pomegranates (female).

KEY 3

THE EMPRESS

This card means:
MATERIAL ABUNDANCE, FERTILITY

Interpretation: Marriage; fertility to would-be parents. Balance and stability. Openness of character and fair dealing. Wealth. Contentment. A fruitful harvest for the farmer; realization of creative projects for those in the arts.

Reversed: Infidelity. Poverty may disrupt the home. Psychological problems may cause instability. War and destruction may come.

In a Reading: If this card comes up in a woman's reading and refers to the future, it can mean that she will have considerable wealth and material possessions or that a child is on the way. If the card indicates the past, perhaps she has had wealth; the cards that follow will indicate if she has been able to hold on to it. Of course, it can also mean that she recently has had a child. If the Seeker is a man, the Empress card can suggest that he will shortly be a father, but it is more likely that his question has to do with his success in life. You can suggest that he will have money and material possessions. If he is a farmer, there will be a plentiful harvest; if his creativity lies in the arts, he will be amply rewarded. In reverse, this is not a good card for either man or woman. Perhaps the question asked concerns the world situation, and then it is possible that war and famine are indicated—either in the past or the future, depending on where the card lies.

Description: The Empress sits on cushions in a fertile garden, a field of ripening wheat before her. The stream flowing between the trees is the Water of Life—the vivifying principle of all that grows. Her scepter shows her domination over the created world, as symbolized by the twelve signs of the Zodiac. The heart-shaped shield at her side is inscribed with the symbol of Venus.

Three is the number of trinity—father, mother, and then the son. The Empress expresses all that is meant by this fruitful union on the material plane. The virgin High Priestess has now become the Earth Mother, the multiplier of images. The subconscious has developed the seed-thought planted in it, and now we have the material results.

THE EMPEROR.

KEY 4

THE EMPEROR

When you see this card think:
LEADERSHIP

Interpretation: Authority, paternity, leadership, government. War-making power. Self-mastery; reason.

Reversed: Loss of self-control. A weak character; bondage to parents. Emotional immaturity. Possible injury or theft.

In a Reading: If the Seeker has not revealed his question, remember that it probably concerns one of the following: work, career, or business; love, marriage, pleasure; trouble, loss, scandal; money, property. From the information in the lesson on how to lay out the cards, and from looking over the whole spread, you will get an idea of the type of question that has been asked. If this card falls in the layout of a woman, it probably concerns a man very close to her. In a reading for a man, the Emperor may mean either the man himself or his superior, perhaps his commanding officer if he is in the army.

In reverse, this card also has many meanings. For a young person, it could mean a father or husband might be injured in battle, or even the boy himself if he is in the armed forces. In this case, do not say he will be injured; instead, suggest he might be put in a position where alertness and common sense would avert disaster. Always try to give your reading a positive tone.

Description: A regal man sits on a throne decorated with rams' heads (emblem of Mars). He is a crowned monarch, commanding and stately. His virile power is indicated by the Crux Ansata, the Cross of Life (also called the Egyptian ankh), which he grasps with his right hand while his left holds a globe of dominion. The background consists of bare, reddish mountains, another symbol of Mars. In Astrology, Venus is the consort of Mars, and in the Tarot, the Emperor is paired with the Empress. His number is Four, which indicates that all is stable, four-square.

The Emperor is the *active* father principle, which has now combined with the *active* mother principle of the Empress and produced the fertile world. The Magician and the High Priestess are the same forces, but remain still in their potential state.

THE HIEROPHANT

KEY 5

THE HIEROPHANT

This card means:
TO BE RULED BY THE CONVENTIONAL

Interpretation: Need to conform. The importance of being socially approved, especially by one's own group. Bondage to the conventions of society. Preference for the outer forms of religion.

Reversed: Unconventionality, unorthodoxy. Take care not to become superstitious. The card of the inventor as well as of nonconformist youth.

In a Reading: If the card is in the future, the Seeker will feel the need to conform to the morals and manners of society. He will like to go to church "just for the music" or to please his parents or the people down the street. If the Hierophant turns up in the past, this attitude is already characteristic of the Seeker. But if the Hanged Man or other spiritual cards come up in the future, it is safe to predict that the present attitude will change to one of more openness to spiritual ideas. In reverse, this card indicates unconventionality like that of the young people of today. There is a warning here that if the Seeker is delving into the occult, he should avoid becoming superstitious and seeing signs and portents in everything around him. If you are asked to read for someone in the ministry, this might be a good card to pick.

Description: It was a Hierophant who was the master of the Eleusinian mysteries, rites that were held once a year near Athens.

Here the Hierophant is seated between pillars repeating the theme of duality, as in the card of the High Priestess. He wears the triple crown of a pipe, and the symbol of Three is repeated in his staff to indicate his rule over the creative, formative, and material worlds. The garments of the kneeling monks are decorated with the white lilies of abstract thought and the red roses of desire. Between them are crossed keys, the keys of the kingdom—one, gold for the sun and the superconscious; the other, silver for the moon and the subconscious.

The Hierophant represents traditional, orthodox teaching considered suitable for the masses. Therefore, he is the ruling power of external religion.

THE LOVERS.

KEY 6

THE LOVERS

The meaning is:
THE CHOICE BETWEEN TWO LOVES OR ATTRACTIONS

Interpretation: Choice between vice and virtue. Temptation. The beginning of romance. Harmony of the inner
and outer life. Inspiration from above. Love uncontami-
nated by great material desire.

Reversed: Infidelity. Interference by in-laws with a marriage. Quarrels over children. The possibility of a wrong
choice; the need to stabilize the emotions.

In a Reading: This is a happy card; it occurs often in
readings for young people. Usually it means the beginning
of romance. It can also mean temptation. Suppose the
card of the Lovers is in the Seeker's past, and another
Queen card appears in the future; there may be jealousy.
  When reversed, this card may mean there is in-law

trouble, but look for other meanings if the Seeker is mature. It could be that a sister or brother, or even a friend living in the Seeker's house, has caused an upset.

Description: A nude man and woman stand beneath the outstretched arms of Raphael, angel of Air, who gives them his blessing. Behind the woman is the Tree of the Knowledge of Good and Evil, bearing five fruits for the five senses; the serpent of sensation is in charge. Behind the man is a tree bearing the trefoil flames of the twelve signs of the Zodiac, each divided into three decans.

This key has deep metaphysical meanings. It indicates that with the conscious mind it is almost impossible for us to reach the superconscious; we must, in meditation or prayer, reach it by way of the subconscious. Here the man, representing the conscious mind and reason, looks to the woman, representing the subconscious mind and the emotions. It is she who can look up at the angel of the superconscious.

Six, the number of the divine force in nature, of cooperation and marriage, fits in with the meanings of this picture. Key 6 in some Tarot packs shows a man trying to choose between an obviously "good" woman and a wanton. There is a Cupid above them with his arrow poised. In reading the cards, either interpretation may be given.

Lesson 9

THE SECOND THIRD

KEY 7

THE CHARIOT

When you see this card, think of:
CONQUEST

Interpretation: Success, victory through hard work; the well-balanced life. Triumph over ill health, money difficulties, or enemies of any sort. A responsible nature. An ability to resist temptation. Travel in comfort.

Reversed: Unbalanced life, uncontrolled passion, leading to downfall. An unethical victory. Ill health. In spite of a desire for change, the journey is postponed.

In a Reading: If this card is in the Seeker's future, it can be read as a conquest to come, perhaps in business or in health. If the Seeker is a farmer or, perhaps, raises dogs or horses, he will be successful.

If this card is in the past, the Seeker has had his

success; the cards that follow indicate if it is a lasting one. They may also show ill health overcome in the past. Reversed, there is a possibility of ill health to come; so tell the Seeker to be sensible about his diet and do everything possible to avoid illness. Never tell anyone he is going to be sick; instead, subtly suggest he should be more careful.

You will notice I repeatedly advise against taking a negative note. Readers have great responsibility in interpreting the cards—if they do not use common sense and positive philosophy, they can do the Seeker damage and cause him unnecessary worry.

Description: A prince rides in a chariot under a starry canopy, carrying the wand of authority and will, with which he must control the sphinxes. The white sphinx is a symbol of mercy, the positive life principle; the black one, a symbol of stern justice and the negative life principle. The prince must maintain a balance between them or they will pull in opposite ways and tear him asunder. The starry canopy indicates that he is under celestial influences that will affect his victory. The front of the chariot bears a Hindu sign of the union of the male and the female; over it are the wings of spirit.

This key signifies victory for one who has conquered and held control of the unruly forces of the emotions and the mind. Seven is the number of work perfected, and the charioteer has accomplished this.

KEY 8

STRENGTH

When you see this card, think of:
TRIUMPH OF LOVE OVER HATE

Interpretation: Triumph of one's higher nature over material desires. Love is always stronger than hate. The ability to bring both sides of one's nature into harmony is here indicated. The Seeker is learning how to release his fears.

Reversed: Domination of the material side of life. Fear of overwhelming passions either in ourselves or in others. Discord in one's affairs. Too much attention is given to the material at the expense of the mental and spiritual.

In a Reading: I always welcome this card when it comes up in a reading because it can teach the Seeker a good bit about the way he has been handling his affairs. A search will usually reveal that he has been trying to *make* things happen by sheer will and determination, instead of applying love and consideration to the problem. This card, in the past, shows that he has handled the situation correctly; if it is in the future, he had best try to bring about a change in his affairs by showing love and consideration. Reversed, of course, it shows that things have been handled badly in the past; in the future it is a definite warning to apply the love and consideration that are so necessary to keep his life running smoothly.

Description: A woman with flowers in her hair and around her waist, with confidence in her powers, closes the lion's mouth. She is exhibiting spiritual courage, for the lion (our strong passions) can turn and rend us if we don't learn how to handle him. She wears the white dress of purity; over her head is the cosmic lemniscate, which proclaims her an adept.

In some decks she is called the Enchantress and so she is, for she needs no physical strength for her purpose. The Number Eight is a symbol of balance—each loop of the 8 is the same as the other. The woman has initiated a spiritual cause and, therefore, according to the laws of the universe, she will receive a spiritual effect. Brute force is never a match for spiritual strength.

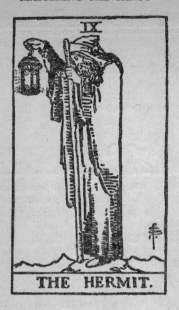

KEY 9

THE HERMIT

The message contained in this card is:
WISDOM OFFERED

Interpretation: Silent counsel; a meeting with one who will guide the Seeker toward his goals. The courage and maturity to do what is right. The openmindedness to be willing to accept help when offered.

Reversed: Wisdom of others spurned. Rejection of one's own maturity. Foolish vices. Refusal to learn and experience new things. Tendency to be a perpetual Peter Pan.

In a Reading: People are often pig-headed and refuse to accept any other way of doing things than their own. If this card comes up in the Seeker's past, then he has been offered some wise advice; the following few cards will show whether he has been able to accept it or not. If the card is in his future, suggest to him that when unselfish help is offered he should not turn it down. If reversed and in the past, it indicates that the Seeker has already refused some help from an older and wiser person; if reversed and in the future, suggest to him that instead of turning down the help that will be offered, he should give the matter further thought to see if the help is of real value to him. This card can also suggest that the Seeker lives in a childish world of his own and refuses to grow up. If the Seeker is a woman, she does not want to act or dress according to her own age, but like a much younger person.

Description: The Hermit stands alone on a snowy mountain peak far above the weary travelers below, for whom he lights the way. His lantern is the Lamp of Truth; it contains the six-pointed star of radiant energy, which suggests, "Where I am, there you may be." He remains on the heights throughout the long nights of spiritual darkness, waiting for those who act, dare, keep silent, and find the way. The card of the Fool is that of a youth looking upward in the morning light, full of expectancy, whereas the Hermit is a bearded ancient looking down at the night. He has arrived at a high point of spiritual wisdom, which he is now willing to share with others.

WHEEL of FORTUNE.

KEY 10

THE WHEEL OF FORTUNE

When you see this card think of:
THE UPS AND DOWNS OF FATE

Interpretation: Fate brings success, the unexpected arrival of good fortune. New conditions in the home or business. The laws of chance are in the Seeker's favor.

Reversed: Luck has deserted the Seeker for the time being. There will be set-backs in his affairs. Courage is required to meet the new conditions, but eventually he will reap what he has sown.

In a Reading: If this card falls in the Seeker's past, you will know he has had an unusual turn of luck and has perhaps built success upon it. If it is in his future, then the luck may be expected within a short time. If this card is near a King, Queen, or Knight, one of the people represented by these cards will have contributed to the turn of fate. If Key 10 is the last card in the spread, then the final outcome of his question seems to be out of his hands. He must simply apply all his knowledge to bring about some fortunate opportunity. When reversed, naturally the Wheel of Fortune is likely to bring setbacks in his plans. In the past, it may mean that his bad luck is over and now he can build toward a better future.

Description: The Wheel of Fortune keeps on turning and carries men and their destinies up and then down. The Number Four occurs several times in relation to this card. Here we see the letters T, A, R, O on the wheel, interspersed with the four letters IHVH for Jehovah. At the four corners of the card are four mystical creatures mentioned in the Bible (Ezekiel 1:10; Revelation 4:7) that correspond to the four fixed signs of the Zodiac: the bull for Taurus, the lion for Leo, the eagle for Scorpio, and the man or angel for Aquarius. They show that spiritual reality is unchanging, though the wheel of personal life turns.

KEY 11

JUSTICE

Overall meaning of this card is:

BALANCED JUDGMENT

Interpretation: Justice will be done. Balance is required in all things. Lawsuits will be won. The balanced personality demands that one get rid of preconceptions and prejudices. Desire for an education that will lead to a well-balanced mind as its objective. The beginning of a new cycle in the Seeker's life, with a good balance between business and home.

Reversed: Injustice, inequality. Legal complications. A biased mind, full of prejudice. Avoid excessive severity.

In a Reading: In a reading the important thing to notice is the scales, which are perfectly balanced in the picture. This card in a Seeker's layout could mean a number of different things. It is up to the Reader to decide which would make the most sense and go along with the meanings of the other cards. Key 11 could mean that the Seeker has won a lawsuit, if it is in the past; or it could suggest that he had handled a matter either in the home or business with balanced judgment. In the future, it would mean a good outcome of a lawsuit, if one was pending, with both parties satisfied.

When reversed and in the past, it may mean that the Seeker has experienced injustice in some matter or even the loss of a lawsuit. Reversed and in the future, it could signify a disastrous lawsuit, and the Reader would be wise to advise against going to court. Then again it may mean a prejudiced mind, either that of the Seeker or, if a court card is present, that of some other person. The Reader must feel his way and not give a definite meaning to the card until, by reading those that surround it, he can get a better picture.

Description: The figure of Justice holds a sword in her right hand, which can cut two ways. In her left are scales to assure that her judgment will be a just one. Behind her are two pillars very similar to the ones seen in the card of the High Priestess and the Hierophant. The fact that she sits between the positive and the negative shows that she will give a well-balanced type of justice. Note that she is not blindfolded, as in present-day cartoons of justice, but has her eyes wide open to see all that is going on, and judge accordingly.

THE HANGED MAN.

KEY 12

THE HANGED MAN

The implication of this card is:
SELF-SURRENDER TO HIGHER WISDOM

Interpretation: Spiritual growth; surrender to a higher wisdom. A complete reversal of one's usual way of life. Dependence no longer on the self but on the Creative Intelligence that runs the universe. Material temptations should be conquered. A period of indecision in one's life. The ability to prophesy to some degree.

Reversed: Preoccupation with the concerns of the self. Absorption in physical matters. Resistance to spiritual teachings. False prophecy.

In a Reading: At first glance, many people are repelled by this card; to them a hanged man means torture and pain. But a closer look shows that there is a look of contentment on the Hanged Man's face, and a halo around his head. In the future of the Seeker, this card means that a time is approaching when he will seek more spiritual instruction. If the card is in his past, he has already done so.

In reverse, this card can mean the Seeker takes such great enjoyment in the physical aspects of life that he has no time to learn he has a soul. In the future, reversed, it means he will not be guided by the wisdom of others nor trust his life to anything but his own wits.

The Hanged Man may also indicate a person who has a gift of prophecy or a type of clairvoyance. When the card is right side up, he uses this gift for good.

Description: The Hanged Man is suspended from a T-cross of living wood, with his arms folded behind his back and one leg crossed behind the other. There is a nimbus about his head, and his face expresses deep contemplation rather than suffering. This figure embodies the idea of the utter dependency of the human personality on the Tree of Cosmic Life. The Key is #12; and we find that here the lower forces of the twelve signs of the Zodiac have been transmuted into the higher, uplifting meanings of the signs. It is a reversal of thought rather than one of body—a silent, unostentatious reversal of one's way of life, combined with a perfect tolerance of other people—the aim of the practical occultist.

KEY 13

DEATH

When you see this card, think of:
CHANGE, REBIRTH, RENEWAL

Interpretation: Renewal, transformation. Birth of new ideas, new possibilities. Destruction of the old, followed by birth of the new.

Reversed: Temporary stagnation; tendency to inertia. Death of a political figure; political upheaval, revolution. Disaster.

In a Reading: It is not only ancient Gypsy tradition but also good modern psychology never to predict death for the Seeker. This is not really a card of death, anyway, but one of renewal. To predict death is a dreadful thing to do—it can lead the Seeker to imagine any small pain or injury is the beginning of the end. A minor complaint will grow larger in his mind, and his whole outlook will be twisted with fear. Therefore, NEVER, NEVER PREDICT DEATH FOR THE SUBJECT OF AN INTERPRETATION. Also, do not predict death for anyone in his family.

When this card comes up in a spread, the first thing to do is calm the Seeker and explain to him the real divinatory meaning of the Death card. If the card comes up in the past, there has already been a type of renewal or change in his way of life. If the card is in his future, then the change will occur shortly. If it is next to a court card, the change will occur through that person.

Description: A skeleton in armor rides a white horse that has trampled over a fallen king and draws close to a child and a young woman. A bishop with his hands raised in prayer awaits the skeleton's coming. Death's banner bears a five-petaled rose, symbol of Mars and the Life-force. The river in the background will flow to the sea, whence the water will be drawn up by the sun into clouds, and then fall on the land into streams and rivers—and again flow out to sea. The symbolism here is the constant circulation of the Life-force that comes into materialization and then flows out again.

This card shows that the patterns of life change from the old to the new; prejudices, manners, morals, and opinions gradually die and are replaced by new ideals and hopes that, in their turn, are discarded.

Lesson 10

THE LAST THIRD

TEMPERANCE.

KEY 14

TEMPERANCE

This card conveys:
ADAPTATION, COORDINATION, TEMPERING INFLUENCES

Interpretation: Adaptation, self-control, modification, coordination; working in harmony with others, the use of successful combinations. Good management and good balance in one's outlook on life. Artistic creations.

Reversed: Bad management; unfortunate combinations; competing interests in business or personal affairs. Lack of good judgment. The creative temperament out of balance.

In a Reading: The word "temperance" may carry in our minds an association with the old Temperance Society, which fought so hard against alcohol. But here its meaning is associated rather with the tempering of steel, the bringing together of two opposite qualities. It is another way of saying *balance,* which, you may have noticed, is a recurring theme of the Tarot. In a reading, this card would indicate that the Seeker was able to bring things together in successful combinations—for example, in a business partnership, in matchmaking, or even in successfully mixing the ingredients of a cake or a party. In cards pointing to the past, it would mean the Seeker had already accomplished something of this sort, and the cards around Temperance will suggest what the combination was.

When Temperance is reversed, the Seeker is not good at putting successful combinations together, or the combinations may be evil, such as introducing two crooks to each other.

Description: Michael, one of the archangels, is pouring the essence of life from the silver cup of the subconscious into the golden cup of the conscious; from the unseen into the seen, and then back again. This represents the entry of Spirit into matter, as well as the flowing of the past through the present and into the future.

The square on the angel's breast is that of four-square reality; the triangle within the square is that of Spirit. This symbol is used as the sign of the Sacred Tarot, of Spirit embodied in flesh. The water in the pool is that of the subconscious mind of man and the universe. Michael is well balanced, with one foot in the water and the other on the dry land of the material universe. At the end of a long path is the crown of attainment and mastery.

KEY 15

THE DEVIL

This card is associated with:
BONDAGE TO THE MATERIAL

Interpretation: Domination of matter over spirit. Temptation; illness; a perverse sexual life. Disregard for human dignity; wrong use of force. Bondage to the material; revolution; black magic.

Reversed: Removing the chains of bondage; overcoming pride and selfishness. Release from the forces of evil. Black magic has no power over the person who seeks help from above. Or this card can indicate a weak and timid person, with a tendency to ineffectuality and indecision.

In a Reading: This should be a helpful card, for it indicates where we have put our dependence—on the material or the spiritual. If this card falls in the Seeker's past, it shows he has been subject to evil influences; the cards next to it indicate whether he has overcome them. A court card would identify the sort of person who exerted this influence. One of the aces would mean that a new beginning is possible. If the Devil shows up in the future, the Seeker will soon be tempted in a wrong direction. The card following will show whether he will resist this temptation. Always, in a case like this, try to persuade the Seeker to resist. Explain that his problem will be easier if he asks for spiritual help; that there is really no profit in wrongdoing.

Reversed, this card means that evil influences have been resisted or overcome. The chains about the nude figures in the card are loose and can be removed at will.

Description: A horned devil with bat's wings, perched on a half-cube, signifies the half-knowledge we have if we rely on only the visible, sensory side of life. His right hand is upraised in the sign of black magic; his left holds an inverted flaming torch of destruction. The inverted pentagram on his forehead is the sign that man's place in the cosmos is reversed and he now has evil intent.

The chained nude figures are similar to those in Key 6. The man's tail represents the wrong use of the signs of the Zodiac; the woman's, the wrong use of the wine of life. We must always remember that there is no devil except of our own creation.

THE TOWER.

KEY 16

THE TOWER

The impact of this card is:
THE OVERTHROW OF SELFISH AMBITION

Interpretation: Selfish ambition is about to come to naught. Conflict, change, unforeseen catastrophe. Old notions upset. Chance of bankruptcy. Overthrow of existing ways of life. Disruption will bring enlightenment in its wake.

Reversed: Same as above, but in lesser degree. The gain of freedom of body or mind, but at great cost. False accusations, false imprisonment; oppression.

In a Reading: If the Seeker has built the tower of his success on shoddy products or methods, or let his ambition run away with him, he is ready for a fall. Warn him that he may face bankruptcy and ruin if he continues in his present course. Pride goeth before a fall, and the fall is coming. If there is a card near the Tower that suggests travel, it may mean a change of residence and a new start if he mends his ways. Court cards will signify the sort of person who may be responsible for his downfall. A spiritual card will show that he has learned his lesson.

In the reversed position, this card means much the same thing—but lesser failures, a less serious fall. A court card near him may mean someone is falsely accusing him of wrongdoing. The Tower can be negative as the end card of a reading, for it indicates that in spite of the Seeker's efforts the result will be a comedown of some sort.

Description: The crown of materialistic thought is struck by the lightning of righteous spirit, and it falls from the tower of purely material ambition. The tower is made of the bricks of traditional race-thought, such as "dog eat dog," "the devil take the hindmost," and that only ruthless dealings will get one to the top. The man and woman are falling from the tower of a too-material existence, to be dashed on the rocks of hard fact below. The lightning is the spiritual truth that breaks down ignorance and false reasoning. "Except the Lord build the house, they labor in vain that build it."

KEY 17

THE STAR

The meaning of this card is:
HOPE, INSPIRATION, HEALTH

Interpretation: Courage, hope, inspiration. Gifts of the Spirit. Health will improve. Unselfish aid. Great love will be given and received. Insight into the meanings of life. No destruction is final.

Reversed: Doubt, pessimism, stubbornness. Lack of perception. Loss of friendship or love. Chance of physical or mental illness.

In a Reading: If the Star falls in the Seeker's future, he will experience many good things, but the cards surrounding it indicate which will be most important to him. Health will improve; there will be new friendships, and the old ones will deepen. A true love will develop that could lead to marriage. In his business or profession, unselfish aid will be given to the Seeker by those around him. If the card falls in his past, he has already had this aid and love and good health, and the cards of his future will tell whether these blessings will continue. If the cards in the future do not seem too good, caution him not only to hope for the best but also to be guided by inspiration and by those who have aided him in the past. The Star, reversed, in either the past or future means the Reader should urge him to use caution. For his health he must watch his diet and get plenty of rest and exercise. His pessimism and doubt may cause something resembling a nervous breakdown. He should be encouraged to read inspirational books, and if he is willing, he should learn something of meditation.

Description: A beautiful maiden kneels with one knee on land and one foot in the water, symbolizing her perfect balance between the subconscious of the water and the dry land of matter. She pours the Waters of Life impartially from two pitchers, and the water poured on earth divides into five rivulets for the five senses. Behind her a bird, said to be the sacred ibis of thought, rests in the tree of the mind. Eight stars, each with eight points, represent radiant cosmic energy.

The Star is the card of meditation, showing us that meditation modifies and changes (transmutes) the personal expressions of cosmic energy as it pours down upon us. If we will but listen, the Truth will unveil itself in the silence.

THE MOON.

KEY 18

THE MOON

This card should make you think of:
CHANGE AND DECEPTION

Interpretation: Unforeseen perils; deception; change. May mean bad luck for an acquaintance. Intuition, dreams, unfoldment of latent powers. The card of the psychic.

Reversed: Imagination will be harnessed by practical considerations. Change will not be disruptive. Deception will be unmasked. Love will win, but not before it is almost destroyed by misunderstandings. No risks should be taken.

In a Reading: This is an interesting card with many meanings on many levels. Be careful in interpreting it—be sure to judge it against the other cards in the spread. In the past of the Seeker, it could mean he has gone through perils he did not foresee. Perhaps he is psychic, and is now developing powers that he only recently discovered within himself. In the future, the Seeker must watch for unseen perils and try to avoid misfortune to someone he knows.

In reverse, the Moon is not really a bad card, since it cancels out the things that are suggested when right side up. It is of great importance if it covers the card of the Seeker, for then it may betoken the development of greater psychic talent. Each card in the spread must always be read in connection with the question asked, unless that is simply, "What will happen to me in the next six months?" Incidentally, that is a good question to suggest to anyone who does not know what to ask.

Description: A dog and a wolf bay at the moon that is both full and in its first quarter. In the foreground is the pool of the subconscious, the great deep of mind-stuff out of which psysical manifestation emerges. The zodiacal sign of the crab is ruled by the Moon. Out of the waters a crayfish crawls, symbolizing the early stages of conscious unfoldment. The wolf is nature's untamed creation; the dog is the result of adaptation to the life of man. The rugged path going off into the distance is the journey we all must take to higher and higher states of consciousness. The Seeker must travel between the towers of good and evil to reach his goal. In its loftiest sense, the Moon relates to the High Priestess and is the keeper of the mysteries of the universe.

THE SUN .

KEY 19

THE SUN

This card means:
ATTAINMENT, LIBERATION

Interpretation: Success, attainment; a good marriage. Achievements in the arts, science, and agriculture. Studies completed. Happiness, pleasure in the simple life, good health.

Reversed: Future plans clouded; trouble in marriage; a broken engagement. Failure is met at every turn. Loss of a valued object.

In a Reading: This is a very good card. Look at the cards around it to determine what kind of success and happiness will come to the Seeker. It can mean a happy marriage or success in business or in the arts, so better feel your way before you make a statement. If the Sun comes after a "bad" card, then you know that the matter will be cleared up. If it comes before such a card, you must remind the Seeker that the Sun gives him the power to overcome the problems in his life.

Description: A huge, brilliant sun shines down upon a naked child astride a horse. The walled garden in back of him is the cultivated garden of Man, which he has now left behind him. Four sunflowers are turned toward him for their fuller development, rather than toward the sun. They represent the four elements: Air, Earth, Fire, and Water. The child is fair, like the Fool, and like him also wears a wreath and red feather. His nakedness indicates he no longer has anything to hide.

The child holds the red banner of the conquest of life in his left hand, the subconscious; he has passed it on from his right, the conscious. This is what we all do with a skill well learned. First we are careful and watch each movement, whether in bicycling or playing the piano; later, we can perform automatically. This is what the child is accomplishing with the forces of life.

The Number Nineteen is considered in mythology and legends as the number of the Sun. One who has attained the age of nineteen becomes a Sun initiate, ready to achieve on the inner plane what the Sun accomplishes in giving life and warmth to the earth.

JUDGEMENT.

KEY 20

JUDGEMENT

This is the card that betokens:
SPIRITUAL AWAKENING

Interpretation: Awakening; renewal. A life well lived, work well done. A change in personal consciousness, which is now on the verge of blending with the universal. Spiritual awakening. Renewed energy, better health, a quicker mind.

Reversed: Fear of death; failure to find happiness. No interest in the spiritual side of life. Possible loss; ill health.

In a Reading: If the Seeker is obviously not a very spiritual type, try to find one of the more practical meanings of this card to fit his situation. If it appears in the future, the Reader may hint at a spiritual awakening to come; if in the past, then the Seeker has already had an awakening of some sort, and the rest of the cards will indicate whether he has followed this up or let it come to naught. In reverse, Judgement indicates a type of failure to lift one's self higher spiritually or materially in such matters as health and creativity. As the last card in a spread, Judgement would mean a good ending of the Seeker's troubles through a more spiritual application to his problems.

Description: A group of people rise from their coffins, which are floating on the sea of the subconscious. They are roused by the angel Gabriel, who blows seven blasts on his trumpet to wake Man from his earthly limitations. The cross on his banner is the solar symbol of balanced forces.

The Number Twenty is composed of two complete cycles of ten, each containing the experience of the nine digits. In Twenty we find a Two before the Zero of unmanifest forces, signifying that the Life-force has now entered into matter and has multiplied.

THE WORLD.

KEY 21

THE WORLD

The thought to hold for this card is:

TRIUMPH IN ALL UNDERTAKINGS

Interpretation: Fulfillment of all desires. Reward; assured success. Freedom to move ahead in all undertakings. The ability to make others happy. Change of home or means of livelihood; travel. Arrival at a state of cosmic consciousness. The path of liberation.

Reversed: Success yet to be won. Fear of change in one's home or profession. Lack of vision. Refusal to learn the lessons of life as shown in the other cards.

In a Reading: This can be called the best card in the deck, and when it appears in a Seeker's layout the Reader can with confidence predict good things of both a material and a spiritual nature. If it is reversed, give encouragement instead of just flatly saying that things will not be too good. As the final card in a spread, it can be terrific. The most important use of the Tarot, it must be remembered, is to make us think.

Description: A dancing maiden, surrounded by a wreath of leaves, is clad only in a scarf. She holds in each hand a magic wand, one representing the power of involution and the other of evolution, which she now possesses. The wreath symbolizes Nature on her regular course; the ribbons around it are suggestive of the cosmic lemniscate. The four animals are those we have met before in the Wheel of Fortune. They represent the four elements and the four signs of the Zodiac. The dancer represents the final attainment of man, the merging of the self-conscious with the subconscious, and the blending of these two with the superconscious. The World implies the final state of cosmic consciousness, the supreme good, to which all the other cards in the Major Arcana have led.

HOW TO READ THE CARDS

Lesson 11

GENERAL OBSERVATIONS

Now that you are familiar with all seventy-eight Tarot cards and their meanings, of course you want to start right in and use them. But before you try your hand at divining, here are some simple rules and suggestions you should bear in mind.

Shuffling:

As you have noticed, the cards have a different meaning when reversed (upside down), and therefore the pack should be mixed so that approximately half the cards are reversed. The way to do this is to divide the pack into two piles, and then point the two piles at each other, narrow ends facing. Shuffle them together as you have seen card experts riffle cards, using the thumbs so that a card falls from each pile alternately. Repeat this shuffle a number of times to mix the cards thoroughly. Naturally, it would not be desirable to have the first card right side up, the second reversed, the third right side up, the fourth reversed, and so on. The reversing should occur at random rather than at regular intervals.

Before each reading, give the cards a good shuffle in this manner. Then hand the pack to the Seeker and ask him to shuffle them in any way he pleases—do *not* try to teach him your method.

Choosing the Significator:

If you have not already decided in your mind which court card to use to represent the Seeker, now is the time to look through the deck and select it. Lay it, face up, in the center of the table. If you find the choice difficult to make, talk it over with the Seeker. Remember that hair and eye color, though helpful, are not crucially important. Naturally, a Page should be chosen to represent a young person, a Queen a woman, and so on. (The possibilities are described in detail at the beginning of Lesson 6, on the court cards.)

The Question:

Questions usually fall under one of the following categories:

1. LOVE, MARRIAGE, FAMILY SITUATIONS
2. MONEY, BUSINESS AFFAIRS, PROPERTY
3. PERSONAL ACCOMPLISHMENT, TRAVEL
4. STATES OF MIND; PROBLEMS ENCOUNTERED ON THE SPIRITUAL PLANE

Ask the Seeker to pick his question and hold it firmly in his mind while he shuffles the cards, the idea being to somehow shuffle the question into the cards. That is, he should concentrate on it exclusively as he shuffles. He is to stop shuffling when he feels he has accomplished this.

Higher forces:

While the Seeker is shuffling, it is well for the Reader to ask, silently, that only the highest spiritual forces be present at the reading, and also that he be guided to give a true and sensible reading.

Two Ways to Ask the Question:

The first way of proceeding is to let the Seeker state his question aloud. In this case, I feel that the Reader may be influenced in his interpretation by the knowledge of what he has been asked, and is therefore less likely to give an impartial reading.

The second way is for the Seeker to keep his question to himself until the reading is over. Then, if he wishes, he may tell it. If the Reader has missed the mark, they can go over the layout together and see where the Reader went off the track.

Laying Out the Cards:

I am told that the following way of cutting the cards is an old Gypsy method:

After the Seeker has finished shuffling, he lays the cards face down on the table and then, with his left hand, he cuts them into three piles to *his* left.

The Reader now picks up the piles one at a time with *his* left hand, picking up the first pile first, then the second, then the last.

Since the cards are always read from the viewpoint of the Reader, I like to have the Seeker sit beside me so that he gets the same view of them that I do. Devise your own method, if you wish, but stick to it.

How to Lay Out the Cards:

I have often been asked whether, in laying out the cards, the Reader pulls them toward himself as he turns them up, or away from him. Naturally this will make no difference in the way they fall, but it would make a difference to take them off the pack sideways. Try holding a pack in your hands now, and see which way is more comfortable for you. You will note that a card that is "right side up" when face down will be reversed when you pull it off the pack and turn it face up.

So often students want to ask serious, life-shaking questions to begin with, and then are upset when the cards give a confused response. The first time a student picks up a violin, he knows he is not ready to give a concert; likewise, the Tarot student must practice many weeks, even months, before he can permit his life or someone else's to be influenced by the cards. Don't be in a hurry to be a modern Mlle Le Normand.* It takes a little time to get acquainted with the cards and have them work and demonstrate all their marvelous possibilities. If the Reader is uncertain about the cards' meaning, the subconscious

* Mlle Le Normand was a celebrated cartomancer in Paris at about the time of the French Revolution, who read the cards with remarkable results to such noted personages as Robespierre, Compte de Provence (who later became Louis XVIII), Danton, and Talleyrand. She also read the cards for the Empress Josephine, who burst into tears when the cartomancer warned her of her divorce. Napoleon had Mlle Le Normand imprisoned twice because he did not like the forecasts she had made about him.

will not know which cards to put where, and the reading becomes ineffectual.

THE ABOVE PROCEDURES ARE TO BE CARRIED OUT BEFORE EACH READING, NO MATTER WHAT METHOD OF LAYING OUT THE CARDS IS USED.

Divination with the Tarot is a responsibility. It must always be remembered that some people are very sensitive and suggestible, and that a negative interpretation of the cards may throw them off balance. Give wise advice, and try intuitively to sidestep the sorrow and the painful places in peoples' lives. By helping others, you will also learn much about yourself and your own problems. Never state that a thing *will* happen; say only that it appears probable in the course of events. The future is in each person's own hands, and no matter what the cards seem to say, EVERYTHING IS SUBJECT TO CHANGE.

The person whose future is to be read seems in some way to influence the cards, and so the shuffling by the Seeker is the essential starting point. To get satisfactory results, it is advisable to make sure he is really in earnest. If a group of people are just trifling with the cards, the results will reflect their irresponsible attitude.

After Laying Out the Cards But Before You Read:

Before you try to read each card, it is well to take a look at the overall picture and try to get an idea of the meaning of the layout in general. Are there several cards of one suit? Several court cards? A few of the Major Arcana? These are all things that must be noted, for they will influence you in deciding how to read the cards separately.

WANDS—	Four or more in a spread will indicate growth and energy.
CUPS—	Four or more will indicate that the question has to do with the emotions—perhaps love, children, pleasure.
SWORDS—	Four or more suggest aggressive ambition, perhaps destructive activities.

PENTACLES—   Four or more will mean a question
                about money, trade, material gain.

COURT CARDS—   Several Wands: a business conference
                Several Cups: a gay company
                Several Swords: conflict
                Several Pentacles: politics, high finance

                Two Kings of any suit: a conference
                Two Queens facing each other: gossip
                Two Knights: a fight
                Two Pages: playful pastimes

MAJOR ARCANA—   Three or four: powerful outside forces
                are at work that will influence the
                Seeker. The outcome is not in his
                hands but in those of others.

After a Doubtful Reading:

If a reading of the cards does not seem to have
answered the Seeker's question completely, and if no final
conclusion can be drawn, it may be well to repeat the
entire process, taking the *tenth* card as the *Significator*
instead of the one previously used. The pack should be
shuffled again by the Seeker, cut three times, and the cards
laid out again. The Reader now asks for clarification of
the question. By this means, a more detailed account of
the outcome may be attained. If the reading is still not
clear, I would advise putting the cards away for that
session and trying again the next day.

Diagram 1—The Keltic Method

Lesson 12

THE KELTIC METHOD OF DIVINATION

I have used this method of divination for a number of years, and I find it by far the best, as well as the simplest, way to lay out the cards and read them. I used this procedure in my other two books on the Tarot. It is presented here in the hope you will find it as useful as I do.

When teaching a class in Florida recently, I had my students pair off to do readings for the first time. After the rather confused session was over, I reminded them not to take their readings seriously, as many factors had been present to prevent the possibility of good readings. When I had finished my comment, I heard a woman exclaim, "Thank God!" Evidently the reading she had received from another student had come up with some pretty frightening things. So, once again, I want to warn you *not* to take seriously the first readings you give; and, in any case, you must explain to the person you are reading for that you are just learning, and therefore your readings are sure to be far from accurate.

Steps to Follow:

1. Pick out the Significator from your pack and place it in the middle of the table.

2. Ask the Seeker to select a question to ask the Tarot. It may be asked silently or aloud, whichever you both prefer. Ask him to "shuffle his question into the cards," concentrating on only one question at a time.

3. While this is being done, you (the Reader) ask that only the highest forces surround you while the reading is taking place and that the truth of the matter will be revealed.

4. The Seeker must now place the cards face down on the table. Then, with his left hand, he cuts the cards into three packs toward the left.

5. The Reader picks up the cards with his left hand, taking up the first pile, then the second, then the last.

NOW YOU ARE READY TO LAY OUT THE CARDS

Following the diagram, place the first card from the top of the pack *face up* on top of the Significator. Next, place the second card across it, according to the diagram. Then put card No. 3 on 3, and so forth. After you have taken off the first ten cards and laid them out in this manner on the table, put the rest aside—they will not be used.

Each number on the diagram has a different meaning, as follows:

No. 1: Represents the general atmosphere that surrounds the question asked; the influences at work around it.

No. 2: (This card, though laid sidewise, is always read right side up, not reversed.) It shows the opposing forces. If it is a good card, it does not oppose but rather helps card No. 1.

No. 3: Shows the foundation or basis of the matter, something that has already become part of the Seeker's experience.

No. 4: Shows an influence or experience that has just passed away or is now on its way out.

No. 5: Something that may happen in the future.

No. 6: Things that will happen in the future, e.g., a meeting, an offer, a person, an influence.

No. 7: Shows the fears the Seeker has about his question.

No. 8: The opinion and influence of family or friends on the matter.

No. 9: Represents the Seeker's own hopes and ideals on the matter.

No. 10: THE FINAL OUTCOME: The tenth card tells what the final outcome will be. It will, of course, be modified and influenced by what has been divined from the other nine cards.

Please go back and reread the section in Lesson 11 called "After Laying Out the Cards But Before You Read." Now that you are getting a general picture of the reading and some notion of the question (if the Seeker has not told you what he has in mind), you can start interpreting each card in turn, beginning with the card in position No. 1. Don't hesitate to refer back to the book to see the exact meaning of a card if you have forgotten. Try to relate each card to the ones preceding and following. If a card just does not make sense with the overall story you are weaving, leave it out for the time being; perhaps it will fit in later.

Often, when telling the final story to the Seeker, you can simply say that such-and-such a card doesn't seem to fit into the picture. He usually replies that he understands what it means—an incident or person that may not have an immediate bearing on the reading, but is nevertheless an important factor in his life.

Tell the Seeker what his future is likely to hold for him in relation to the question asked, the negative influences that he must watch out for, and the good influences of which he must take advantage.

Should it happen that the last card is one from which no final conclusion can be drawn, it may be well to repeat the entire operation, following the directions in Lesson 11, under the section "After a Doubtful Reading." If, after the second reading, no better conclusion can be drawn, it is best not to try any more that day. Evidently there is some interference that spoils the reading—or perhaps the answer to the question has not yet been resolved in the unseen.

Lesson 13

TWO SAMPLE READINGS (KELTIC)

We are often tempted when reading a story in a book or magazine to flip over the pages and see how it comes out. Here, however, if you really want to develop your own skill, I suggest you do not look at my interpretation until you have selected the same ten cards, laid them out in the Keltic form of cross and staff, and then read the question and tried to answer it yourself. After that, you may look and see whether you have interpreted the cards in much the same way, or differently.

READING FOR THE ARTIST, PENNY:

I chose the Queen of Cups for Penny, even though her hair is dark brown, because she is a sensitive, artistic person. She had just been offered a job as an art teacher in a college in another part of the state. *Should she accept?*

Here are the cards that came up:

Position 1: Seven of Cups, reversed
Position 2: Nine of Wands, reversed
Position 3: Ace of Wands
Position 4: Five of Pentacles
Position 5: Nine of Cups, reversed
Position 6: Three of Wands, reversed
Position 7: Two of Pentacles
Position 8: Three of Cups
Position 9: King of Cups
Position 10: Two of Swords, reversed

THE READING

1. *Seven of Cups, reversed:* Means a good use of determination and will, a project about to be realized. Penny had told me her question before she shuffled; and, knowing her, I understood that she had been casting around for all sorts of possibilities in the way of employment. Therefore, I saw that the basis of her question was in that area and the job was the "project about to be realized."

2. *Nine of Wands:* As this card is not in opposition to the Seven of Cups, reversed, it means she is well prepared for the job but there will be a struggle before it is hers. She has, however, the good health and obstinacy to see it through.

3. *Ace of Wands:* The beginning of an enterprise, creation, or invention. This card was in the position of the past; it is the basis of the matter, and so it obviously related to the new job offer made a few weeks before the reading.

4. *Five of Pentacles:* This card may mean material trouble, loneliness. That was what was going out of Penny's life. I believed she had been lonely and that the material trouble had been that she had had just barely enough money to live on.

5. *Nine of Cups, reversed:* This card means mistakes, imperfections in present plans, overindulgence in food and drink. It could also be a warning that the job would not be as good as she hoped it would be. As Penny is overweight, it might also be a warning not to overindulge in the future.

6. *Three of Wands, reversed:* Note how many reversed cards there were in this spread. On the whole, this is not a good sign, but it has no dire meaning here. Position 6 concerns the near future, what is going to happen. Here again is a warning against being disappointed. Perhaps before a contract was signed, someone else would be chosen for the position.

7. *Two of Pentacles:* This means harmony in the midst of change; agility in handling situations. New projects are

difficult to launch. As this card was in the position representing her fears, I read it as meaning that Penny was wondering whether she was handling the situation well, as the job seemed difficult to pin down.

8. *Three of Cups:* The conclusion of a matter in plenty. Position 8 represents those around the Seeker, what they think of Penny's new job offer. It would seem that they were pleased and believed it would turn out well.

9. *King of Cups:* A man with light brown hair and hazel eyes, interested in the arts and disposed to be friendly to the Seeker. Penny told me this might be the man she had talked to at the college. It would seem that he might help her get the job.

10. *Two of Swords, reversed:* Release; movement of affairs, sometimes in the wrong direction. Caution against dealing with rogues. This was the last and final card, to which outcome all the other cards had been leading.

The Reader must always be careful to encourage the Seeker in striving for the best possible solution to the problem. So instead of ending on a discouraging note, I told Penny that there would be a release offered to her. But, at the same time, I reminded her that several of the cards had warned against double-dealing and that she must look over the contract carefully, and also assure herself that working and living conditions at the college would meet with her approval.

READING FOR A COLLEGE JUNIOR, MAC:

Mac has dark hair and eyes, is active and restless, so I chose the Page of Swords as his Significator. A young man of about twenty, he is still in college, but he is not happy there nor is he pleased with institutions of learning in general. His question was one that is in the minds of a good many young people today: *Should he join a commune or stay in college?* He told me he knew of a group that wanted to form a community, rent a farm, grow organic vegetables, and lead a "back-to-nature" life of freedom from social restraints.

Pick the following cards from your Tarot pack and lay them out in the Keltic method. Then try your hand at reading the answer to Mac's question, comparing your reading with the one given here.

Here are the cards that came up:

Position   1: High Priestess
Position   2: Two of Cups
Position   3: Eight of Cups
Position   4: Seven of Cups, reversed
Position   5: King of Pentacles, reversed
Position   6: The Hanged Man, reversed
Position   7: The Sun, reversed
Position   8: Seven of Swords
Position   9: Three of Swords
Position 10: Knight of Wands

THE READING

1. *High Priestess:* Position 1 governs the general atmosphere that surrounds the question. The High Priestess signifies hidden influences at work; duality. It is a card of value for the mystic. As it fell in this layout, it seemed to indicate that Mac was of two minds as to what to do—stay and finish college, or join the group. Every hour of the day this question lived in his consciousness as he searched for the answer.

2. *Two of Cups:* The beginning of a love affair or partnership. I asked Mac if he had met an attractive girl recently and had been dating her. He said he had, but as she was not interested in the idea of a commune, he did not want to become too involved with her. If his answer had been no, then this card could have been interpreted as meaning a partnership with the commune group.

3. *Eight of Cups:* Abandoning the present situation; disappointment in love; leaving material success for something higher. As I knew his question, I chose the last meaning, for Mac really did feel that the community farm would be a higher, more idealistic way of life than finishing college and looking for a job.

4. *Seven of Cups, reversed:* Note that these last three cards were Cups, indicating that Mac had a very emotional nature; that he liked pleasure and beauty more than

the cut-and-dried business side of life. This seven was reversed, suggesting that though he had asked a question of the Tarot, he had already begun to develop a mind of his own.

5. *King of Pentacles, reversed:* This card is in the position of what may happen in the future, but since the card presents a man, I surmised it must represent Mac's father, a black-haired man, a chief of industry, who was now coming into the picture.

6. *The Hanged Man, reversed:* From the several meanings of this card in the reverse, I chose that of preoccupation with the ego. For it appeared to me that Mac was intent on pleasing himself; that he wanted what *he* wanted, and was even a little arrogant about it. This card is in the position of the future, so Mac's actions are likely to be based on this attitude.

7. *The Sun, reversed:* Meaning future plans clouded; broken engagement; failure met at every turn. Seven is the position of the Seeker's fears. Was Mac afraid he would not be able to graduate if he stayed in college? Was he secretly worried that the new venture would eventually turn out badly, leaving him with his deals smashed and no qualification for a career in the business world? Perhaps he was also a little sorry that he must break off with the new girl to whom he was attracted.

8. *Seven of Swords:* The card on the eighth position represents what the family—in this instance, Mac's father—thinks of his plan. The Seven of Swords means unstable effort, a plan that may fail.

9. *Three of Swords:* This is the position of the Seeker's hopes, but the card's meanings are sorrow, tears, separation. How do we fit this card into the picture? Does he want assurance of love from his parents and the girl, to be sure they care enough for him to feel great disappointment at the course he is planning? How did you read this card?

10. *Knight of Wands:* This card's meanings are departure, absence, change of residence. The tenth position is that of the final outcome, so in this case the answer to Mac's question is obviously that he will join the commune.

I might have counseled Mac to stay in college, but I decided against it. That would be the conventional thing for an older person to advise and it was what his father had been· doing, and Mac seemed to have pretty well made up his mind against it. Besides, a year or so of another kind of living might be a good experience for him—might, in the end, lead to his finding himself and learning what he really wanted to do with his life.

Lesson 14

THREE QUICK WAYS TO READ

1. *A QUICK YES OR NO*

Sometimes we want just a simple yes-or-no answer to a simple question, such as:

Will Mr. Brown come to the meeting tomorrow?
Will I sell the house?
Is Johnny going to write to me?
Will I go to Europe this summer?

The quick yes-or-no answer is a good method to try when you don't want to spend time and effort for the Keltic or Horoscope methods, both of which are much more complete and go into a question in detail, often showing hidden causes and influences that affect our lives.

Shuffle the question into the cards as before; cut them into three piles to the left, and then pick up first the first pile laid down. Spread all seventy-eight cards out on the table face down. Next, intuitively pick three of them and discard the rest. Turn these three face up. The answer depends on how many of the three are right side up. If all three are, then there is a definite YES answer to your question. If only two are right side up, the answer is a qualified YES. Three cards, reversed, indicate a definite NO, two, reversed, a qualified NO.

2. *THREE ACES SPREAD*

If you want a little more information than just a yes or

no, use this method. Aces are always important cards and can tell you a great deal about such questions as:

Should I marry Jane?
Should I take a partner into my business?
Will my inheritance come through as expected?
Will Mother's health improve?

The pack is shuffled and cut as before. The Reader deals the cards into a pile, face up, no more than thirteen cards, stopping when an ace turns up. He then starts a new pile to the left and follows the same procedure, stopping at an ace, but not dealing out more than thirteen cards if no ace appears. For the third pile, he follows the same procedure. (The rest of the cards are laid aside.) If no aces have been turned up in the three piles, the question is one that the Tarot cannot answer at present. If one or two piles contain no aces, it indicates a waiting period before the matter is solved. If only one ace comes up, it will contain the answer. If aces top more than one pile, the ace on the right contains the first part of the answer; the ace or aces at the left, the final outcome.

EXAMPLE

Question: Should I take a partner into my business?

The cards came up in this fashion, reading from right to left:
(3) Ace of Swords, reversed; (2) No Ace; (1) Ace of Cups

The Ace of Cups indicates that at present the Seeker feels a partnership would be a very good thing. It would presumably bring prosperity to the business, and because the card is a Cup, there should also be harmony between the partners. The absence of an ace in the middle pack suggests there should be a definite waiting period before a decision is made. The Ace of Swords, reversed, would indicate that after waiting, it would be found that the person selected would want too much power and authority in the business and would try to run it his way, which (the card indicates) would lead to disaster.

3. SIX-CARD HUNGARIAN METHOD

This method gives more information than the two preceding ones, but is still in a rather simple form. If the Three Aces Spread has not given you enough information about the question, you might try this one. Shuffle as before, and cut the cards into three piles. Now turn the piles face up. This will give you three of your cards. From the bottom of each pile take the bottom card and place it face up, just above the pile from which you have taken it.

The two cards at the right are the past.
The two cards at the left are the future.
The two middle cards are important—they represent present attitudes.

EXAMPLE

Question: Will Mother's health improve?

The cards came up like this:

Knight of Wands	Page of Wands, reversed	Ten of Swords
Nine of Pentacles	Six of Swords, reversed	King of Cups

Here we find three court cards: a King, Page, and Knight. These people will have an influence on the question.

Cards of the Past
    Ten of Swords: This card shows the woman's recent state of pain and affliction.
    King of Cups: Here is a man in the arts and sciences, probably her doctor. Through his kindness and generosity, as well as his skill, he has been helping her in every way he can.
Cards of the Present
    Page of Wands, reversed: This card can mean a boy or girl in some way connected with the mother. Ask the Seeker if there is such a person in the family. Pages can also simply mean a message, and as the

card is reversed, possibly a discouraging one about
the mother's health.

Six of Swords, reversed: No immediate way out of
difficulties. Possibly this was the message the Page of
Wands brought. This is the attitude of the family at
the present time.

Cards of the Future

Knight of Wands: (The Reader, in this spread, may
take either the top or bottom card of the spread to
read first.) This Knight can create rivalry. Therefore
I would say that a new and younger doctor has been
brought into the case, creating conflict because his
ideas of treatment differ from those of the older
doctor, represented by the King of Cups.

Nine of Pentacles: This is a good card—it definitely
predicts that the mother will recover, for it means
well-being as well as successful accomplishment. She
will live to enjoy her garden and the pleasures of life.

(Note: Under each of the seventy-eight Tarot cards
interpreted in this book there is a variety of meanings, as
you will have observed. It is up to the Reader to select
those that are appropriate for the question posed. In the
case above, the Nine of Pentacles is not read as wealth or
inheritance, but meanings are chosen that fit the situation.
This does not mean that the mother will not enjoy all the
benefits listed under the card.)

Lesson 15

THE TAROT AND ASTROLOGY

The Tarot cards, as we have seen, have many astrological symbols woven into their designs. It is obvious that the originators of the cards were well acquainted with Astrology, as indeed they were with all the occult teachings practiced in the Middle Ages. The Tarot thus has come to seem like a book of wisdom incorporated into separate cards by the sages who worked on the secrets buried in them. But to the average person, and even to people in court circles, they appeared to be merely the cards of a game of chance or a method of fortune-telling. It was a wonderful way for the wise men to pass on their esoteric messages from town to town and country to country, since those who transported the cards had no idea of their secret meanings.

Though the Tarot and Astrology are both used for divination, their methods differ, the latter having a more precise basis in that the hour, day, and place of birth of the Seeker are essential in order to cast a proper horoscope. But they are similar in that the Astrologer consults the meanings of the stars in their particular formations for the Seeker, and the Tarot Reader consults the cards as they fall in the Seeker's spread. To attain a high level of interpretative success in either of these arts, a psychic sense or intuition is a great help.

There is some agreement among masters of the Tarot as to how close the resemblance is. Some go so far as to assign a specific astrological sign to each one of the Major Arcana. But it must be kept in mind that the Tarot is a distinct discipline in itself. Its symbols have descended from many other occult traditions, giving it a more universal meaning and application.

It must also be remembered that when Court de Gébelin first rediscovered the cards in the south of France, they were being used for fortune-telling, and at that time he could find no one who could tell him their inner meanings. This is what the occultists of the ensuing centuries have been trying to do—explore the endless storehouse of their symbolism. It must be remembered, too, that the designs of the cards de Gébelin found were those of the Marseilles deck—much older and cruder in execution than the Waite pack used in this book. The symbols were therefore more difficult to decipher.

A. E. Waite was a member of the Hermetic Order of the Golden Dawn, a secret society in England whose members spent their time in reviving the practices of occultism and Alchemy and delving deeply into the meanings of the Tarot, Astrology, and Numerology. It was from this vast store of knowledge that the astrological symbols were incorporated into Waite's cards. Unfortunately, Waite merely hints at all these correspondences in his book *The Pictorial Key to the Tarot*. Paul Foster Case, who was also a member of the Golden Dawn, in his book, *The Tarot*, has gone into this correspondence between other occult systems and the Tarot. Though it is not spelled out for the neophyte, the serious Tarot student, particularly if he knows some Astrology, will find Case's book a gold mine of information.

CORRESPONDENCES BETWEEN THE MAJOR ARCANA AND THE SIGNS OF THE ZODIAC

THE SUN, Key 19—ARIES

Aries, the first of the twelve signs of the Zodiac, is known as the ram and is a Fire sign. It signifies positive leadership, people who are at their best when they can control and govern themselves as well as others. The Sun is in its exaltation in Aries, giving energy, action, and life. We have assigned Aries to the Tarot Sun.

THE HIEROPHANT, Key 5—TAURUS

Taurus is the sign of the bull and is of the element Earth, the sign of a materialist who is not without a trace of spiritual quality. The Hierophant utilizes material things for spiritual progress, and though in a position of spiritual authority, is the good shepherd in a materialistic sense. At the back of his chair or throne, on either side, is a pair of bull's horns, partly disguised, but there is a hint here to the discerning. We have assigned Taurus to the Hierophant.

THE LOVERS, Key 6—GEMINI

Gemini, the twins, suggest equilibrium, and though the implication is duality, the twins remain together. It is also an Air sign, indicating the exchange of ideas, affection, and sympathy. Raphael is an angel of the Air who, by sending down his light, balances the masculine and feminine, the positive and negative, aspects of the Lovers. We have assigned Gemini to the Lovers.

TEMPERANCE, Key 14—CANCER

Cancer, a water sign, is known as the crab, but its zodiacal symbol is made up of two small suns, each connected with a crescent moon like a cup or bowl. The upper cup is inverted, pouring water into the lower one, just as in Temperance, where the angel is pouring the Water of Life into the lower cup of material experience. Because of this we have assigned Cancer to Temperance.

STRENGTH, Key 8—LEO

Leo, known as the lion, is a Fire sign. It is creative, dominant, and it is ruled by the Sun. It carries the qualities of courage, compassion, faith, rulership, and domination. The lion, though an emblem of violence and cruelty, has darkness, evil, and ignorance as its enemies. Leo draws things to it, as does the woman in Key 8. This card represents the dueling forces of our own natures, the womanly or spiritual side here dominating the baser forces shown by the lion. We have assigned Leo to Strength for this reason.

THE HERMIT, Key 9—VIRGO

Virgo, known as the virgin, is a sign of honesty, chastity, and purity. She is receptive and intuitive, and can renounce rewards as she works for others. These are the qualities of the Hermit, who holds his lantern aloft to light the spiritual path for others. Virgo is the sign of those who seek an ideal and are not content until it is found. We have assigned Virgo to the Hermit.

JUSTICE, Key 11—LIBRA

Libra is known as the scales. It speaks of the justice that presides internally, though the fortunes of men and empires may tip the delicate balance of the scales temporarily. It is the sign of law, justice, balance, and wisdom. It is also the exponent of rebellion against conservatism, and it espouses progressive movements. It is ruled by Venus (Key 3, the Empress), so we also have here the love of culture and beauty. Justice, holding her scales, is an ideal Libran figure, so we have assigned Libra to Justice.

JUDGEMENT, Key 20—SCORPIO

Scorpio, a water sign, is known as the scorpion. It is a dual sign, meaning regeneration as well as belonging to the sign of Death, the Eighth House. Scorpio also stands for the creative energy of sex being sublimated to new ideals and new beginnings. Scorpio is ruled by forceful Mars; thus Gabriel's seven-note trumpet blast arouses those who have slept on the sea of the subconscious and fills them with energetic conscious activity. We have assigned Scorpio to Judgement.

THE CHARIOT, Key 7—SAGITTARIUS

Sagittarius is known as the archer, and is a sign of the rulership of reason and the intellect. It denotes a restless search for new fields to conquer. The Chariot shows just such a man in charge of the chariot of his life and the twin sphinxes of his emotions and reason.

THE DEVIL, Key 15—CAPRICORN

Capricorn, an Earth sign, is known as the goat. It is a negative sign meaning conniving actions, changeableness, capriciousness, coupled with a great desire for wealth and power. Capricorn denotes a person who can be enslaved by sex and material pleasures, just as are the two nude figures in Key 15. The goat horns of the Devil give added evidence of the correspondence between this card and the sign Capricorn, so we have assigned them to each other.

THE STAR, Key 17—AQUARIUS

Although an Air sign, Aquarius is known as the water bearer. The sign is altruistic and helpful, with knowledge of how to handle people and to spread ideas with altruistic intent. How like the figure in Key 17, who pours the energy-giving Waters of Life upon the subconscious as well as the consciousness of all mankind!

THE MOON, Key 18—PISCES

Pisces, a Water sign, is the twelfth and last sign of the Zodiac. It is known also as the fishes. It represents the dual nature of man; it is feminine, receptive, silent, and passive. Those born under this sign are often intuitive, mystical, and psychic. The symbol of Pisces is two cresent moons, back to back, held together by a band at the middle representing man's finite consciousness linked to the infinite cosmic consciousness. Pisces is the most psychic of Astrological signs, and the Moon is the most psychic of the Tarot cards; their meanings blend in suggesting a pathway strewn with temptations as man travels upward on the long journey.

CORRESPONDENCES BETWEEN THE MAJOR ARCANA AND THE PLANETS

THE HANGED MAN, Key 12—SUN

The Sun is the center of the solar system and has the attributes of nobility, sincerity, and the creative urge that betokens leadership. It represents the life-giving force without which nothing could live on earth. It is masculine and powerful, and all creatures turn to it for warmth and all planets revolve around it. To Man, the Sun also symbolizes the sustaining Force of the Universe—God. The Hanged Man is suspended from a tree of living wood, showing his dependence upon nature and the life-giving force. The Number Twelve pertains to the Great Work, triumph over the human personality by the individual. In reversing his way of life, the Hanged Man shows he is now dependent on Spirit—God. We have assigned the Sun to the Hanged Man.

THE HIGH PRIESTESS, Key 2—MOON

The Moon has dominion over the tides and over clear,

pure, virgin water; it brings fruitfulness to things under its spell. The Moon, changeable and fluctuating, is associated with the subconscious as the Sun is with the conscious. The High Priestess, also thought of as Diana, the Moon Goddess, wears on her head a crown of the moon in its phases and keeps some things hidden as does moonlight. We have assigned the Moon to the High Priestess.

THE MAGICIAN, Key 1—MERCURY

Mercury is the planet that deals with man, the thinker; it is mental, logical, and stands for intellectual inquiry, skill, and imagination. It has been called the link between spirit and matter, as is the mind of man. The Magician represents the first step in the coming-down of Spirit from the Fool, that essence which existed before human thought. We have assigned Mercury to the Magician.

THE EMPRESS, Key 3—VENUS

Venus has been called the Mother Goddess, for she is fruitful, humane, harmonious, and beautiful. The symbol of Venus is the circle above the cross that we can see in the heart-shaped shield at the side of the Empress. Venus is not only fruitfulness and productivity but also love and the emotions, and these same attributes belong to the Empress; therefore we have assigned them to each other.

THE TOWER, Key 16—MARS

Mars is the planet of force and energy, good or bad according to the way it is used. Mars is constructive, ambitious, the planet of builders. Its symbol is the cross above the circle, the opposite to that of Venus, showing that the Mars force works almost entirely with material conditions. The constructive force brings on holy wars, as well as destructive wars of aggression. In the Tower we see that the force is that of spiritual lightning used as a corrective. We have assigned Mars to the Tower.

THE EMPEROR, Key 4—JUPITER

Jupiter has been called the lordly planet, the nature of which is to unfold outwardly toward pure reason. Jupiter has the noble attributes of sincerity, benevolence, charity; it is dignified, has determination and leadership. Mars in good aspect to Jupiter elevates the aspiration. In the

Emperor, a lordly figure, we have the same qualities, and therefore we have assigned Jupiter to it.

DEATH, Key 13—SATURN

Saturn's influence is commonly called evil, but in reality there is no evil, since all things work together for ultimate good. Saturn is the planet of limitations, restrictions, and adversities—all that is associated with things in their most earthly aspect. Saturn is also the redeemer, for it stimulates, through adversity, all efforts toward betterment and perfection on the material plane. Death, as depicted in Key 13, not only destroys but also transforms and renews, as symbolized by the river behind the figures. The rising sun is in the distance also to symbolize the constant renewal of life. We have assigned Saturn to Death.

THE THREE THAT ARE LEFT OVER

There are twelve signs of the Zodiac and seven planets, a total of nineteen, but as there are twenty-two cards in the Major Arcana, we have three cards left over—the Fool, the Wheel of Fortune, and the World. Modern Astrology takes into consideration the three new planets—Uranus, Neptune, and Pluto; but in the Middle Ages, when the Tarot was conceived, these planets were not yet known. So the mystics of that day must have dealt with the three remaining cards in another fashion.

In my recent book *A Complete Guide to the Tarot,* I first associated the Tarot with the Tree of Life of the Kabalah before going into the astrological correspondences of the Major Arcana. In this way each of the Major Arcana became part of a trinity composed of a card, a globe, or Sephirah on the Tree of Life, and a planet or zodiacal sign. Here we do not go into the matter so deeply; therefore a simpler explanation must suffice.

At the very top of the Tree of Life is a Sephirah called Kether, and its meaning is pure being, the all-potential, but still not activated as in the remaining Sephiroth. This is where I placed the Fool, as he is also Spirit in its potential, not yet descended into manifestation. Since we have already assigned the planets and signs of the Zodiac, the only remaining astrological symbols are the Nebulae, not yet fixed in their orbits. We have assigned the Fool to the Nebulae.

The Sephirah, Chokmah, is the essence of all wisdom, a power that flows out to all the twelve signs of the Zodiac, embodying them all. Here I have placed Key 21, the World, which is also the epitome of all the Major Arcana. We have assigned the World to the Zodiac in its entirety.

The Wheel of Fortune has been assigned to Malkuth on the Tree of Life, the very bottom Sephirah, the material world that the attributes of the other Sephiroth have been leading down to through their various forces. Here also are found the elements of Air, Fire, Water, and Earth, now in condensed form. These same elements appear in the four corners of the Wheel of Fortune to the four elements, as well. The vicissitudes of fortune, the ups and downs of luck or fate, are about as low on the tree as man can get; here he stays until he awakens and starts the upward journey back to his Father's house where the ring, the robe, and the fatted calf await him.

Lesson 16

LIFE READING
BY THE HOROSCOPE METHOD

This method is not very practical for a reading that requires answers to specific questions. When you want to read for a definite answer, it is better to use the Keltic method or the three simple ways suggested for quick answers. The method that follows could be described as a "life reading," to be used when personality traits and character analysis are desired.

The person who has made a study of Astrology will find this type of reading of particular interest, but it can be used by anyone who follows the directions and correlates the meanings of the cards with those of the Houses upon which they fall. Interesting insights will occur, and some future events or relationships may be predicted, but I have not found the system as practical as the Keltic readings.

The usual beginning steps are as follows: A Significator is chosen for the Seeker and laid in the middle of an imaginary circle. The Seeker shuffles the cards and cuts them; then the Reader takes them up and lays the first card from the top of the pack, face up, on the position of the First House, the second card on the Second House, and so on to the twelfth. The rest of the pack is put aside and not used.

Each House is assigned to departments of life and given allotments of earthly assets and experiences. These are listed below, and are also to be found abbreviated in Diagram 2. Starting with Aries in the First House, try to correlate the card that has fallen there with the meanings of Aries; the second card, with the meanings of Taurus, and so forth.

SOLAR HOUSE	RULER	MEANING IN DIVINATION
1.	ARIES	Aries rules all beginnings; it is assigned to the Seeker's physical appearance and characteristics, his temperament and personality; also his outlook on the world and his potential.
2.	TAURUS	This is the sign that conserves and builds. Concerns financial affairs, the Seeker's earning power and tangible assets.
3.	GEMINI	This is a mental sign that links people together through similar thought. It is assigned to relatives, especially brothers and sisters. It also means communications, such as letters, writings, and short journeys.
4.	CANCER	The Fourth House begins at the point of midnight; it is therefore assigned to all endings. Old age, old people, the father, the first home environment.
5.	LEO	This House governs the heart. Love affairs, children, things that cause excitement such as theatres, gambling, speculations, and also the Seeker's creative ability.
6.	VIRGO	This House rules the general health of the Seeker, also food and hygiene. It rules work and employees as well.

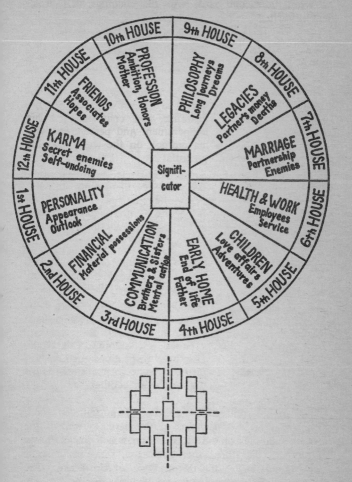

Diagram 2—The Horoscope Method

7.	LIBRA	This House rules both marriage and business partners, dealings with the public, lawsuits, open enemies.
8.	SCORPIO	Rules death, legacies, taxes, also one's partner's money and occult experiences.
9.	SAGITTARIUS	Rules law, philosophy, ideals, and religion. Also dreams, intuition, education, and long journeys.
10.	CAPRICORN	Public life, profession, fame, and social status. The mother of the Seeker is suggested here. Sometimes this is reversed, the mother occupying the Fourth House and the father the Tenth; whichever parent is the provider should occupy the Tenth House.
11.	AQUARIUS	This House rules friends, groups, clubs to which the Seeker belongs. Hopes, wishes, aspirations.
12.	PISCES	Hidden limitations that restrict the Seeker's power of expression, such as Karma. Secret desires, secret enemies, self-undoing. This House also rules institutions such as hospitals, jails, reformatories—places that restrict or confine.

As you interpret each card, it is important to search among the several meanings of the card, as well as the several meanings of the House upon which it has fallen, and try to find those that correspond and make some sense in relation to the life and age of the Seeker. The following may help you understand what is meant.

If, for example, the Five of Swords fell on the Seventh House, Libra—that of marriage, partnerships, and enemies—it would certainly indicate that someone was trying to ruin the Seeker's marriage or his relationship with his business partner. If, however, it fell on the Second House, Taurus, it would indicate that it was a financial loss—

money, jewelry, household goods—and had happened through some type of unfairness or failure on someone's part.

Let us assume that the Three of Cups has fallen on the Eighth House, Scorpio; it would be interpreted as a happy outcome, such as the receiving of a long-awaited legacy or a tax matter cleared up. The same card in the Third House, Gemini, could indicate a celebration with brothers and sisters.

Here is a reading I recently did for Wendy, a sixteen-year-old girl who was having a very hard time both at school and at home. Her father lived in a distant city, and her mother worked to support Wendy, an older brother, and a younger sister. Wendy felt that her brother was favored by both her father and mother. He was given a car of his own and had great freedom. He also continually sided with her mother in restricting Wendy's social activities, sometimes shoving her into a corner and beating her up to prove he was the man of the family. Wendy hated high school, felt she was taking subjects of no interest, which she would never need in her life. She had also lost interest in the games, clubs, and organizations at school, and she disliked the thought of the one year that remained before she could graduate. Her great desire was to go to a different high school for her last year, far away from her mother and the constant bickering. Any tentative plans she made were immediately quashed by her mother, who declared she wanted her daughter at home. We discussed the possibility of a year at a boarding school that might have a scholarship for which she could apply. After our conversation Wendy went home. I then laid out the Tarot for her to see if I could get any clarification on the subject.

A READING BY THE HOROSCOPE METHOD

I chose the Page of Cups as the Significator for Wendy, and placed it in the center of a large imaginary circle. Then I shuffled and cut the cards, and dealt them in a circle around the Significator, putting the first card face up to the left, on Aries, the First House on the diagram. I followed with the rest of the twelve cards, moving to the right, and put the remainder of the deck aside. This is the reading I got.

1. *ARIES:* Looking at the diagram, and checking with the list of zodiacal signs on an earlier page, I saw that Aries means physical appearance, temperament, outlook on the world. *JUDGEMENT* was the card that fell here, meaning a change in personal consciousness, an awakening. Aries and Judgement together must mean that Wendy's personality and temperament were going to change for the better. She could learn to handle situations at home if she used more diplomacy than before.

2. *TAURUS:* Concerns financial affairs. *NINE OF CUPS* fell here. This is the "wish" card. It would indicate that Wendy might get her wish to have her last high school year away from home, and that somehow the money would be found to make it possible.

3. *GEMINI:* This House concerns brothers, sisters, communication. *EIGHT OF WANDS* is approach to a goal. Hence Wendy might find communication with her brother becoming possible. I say brother because her younger sister did not seem to come into the picture. Wendy's goal, it would seem, should be arrived at shortly.

4. *CANCER:* From the meanings of this House, I had to select those pertinent to the situation, so I chose the father. *THE STAR,* reversed, which fell here, indicates that Wendy's father was stubborn and lacked perception. The early home environment was one of constant bickering. The son had seen his father use force to get his own way and he now followed his father's example.

5. *LEO* is the House that governs the heart, matters that cause excitement. *THE MOON,* reversed, fell here. In reverse, it indicates imagination harnessed to practical matters. Storms are weathered, but at a cost, and no risks should be taken. As related to Wendy, it would seem she should not take the risk of upsetting her major desire by running around too much with the boys she knows. With the Moon, reversed, she should be able to be more practical in her outlook.

6. *VIRGO* concerns health, food, and work. *THE DEVIL* indicated she must be extra careful to eat properly balanced meals and get plenty of rest. Again, she needed to be cautioned not to look for sensational experiences, which, in the case of a sixteen-year-old girl, would be

activities such as drinking, taking drugs, or going on wild rides or parties.

7. *LIBRA* is the House of Marriage and partnerships, lawsuits, and open enemies. Falling on this House, the *KNIGHT OF PENTACLES* indicates a young man with dark hair who, at first glance, might be Wendy's brother; the Knight of Pentacles, however, accepts responsibility and likes work and is trustworthy. It seems unlikely that her brother would change so quickly, so the Knight must be someone who will come into Wendy's life and help her with her goal.

8. *SCORPIO* rules death, legacies, and occult experiences. Here, the *KNIGHT OF SWORDS* means a brown-haired, domineering young man. This card can also mean the coming or going of a matter. Perhaps a relative will leave Wendy a legacy and there will be unforeseen conflict concerning it—possibly with her brother.

9. *SAGITTARIUS* rules law, philosophy, and ideals; also intuition and long journeys. *TEN OF CUPS*, reversed, fell here. It could mean loss of friendship. Is it possible that Wendy may lose one of her friends because of her ideals and philosophy of life?

10. *CAPRICORN* is the House of profession and fame; also is the House of the mother. Here, the *TEN OF PENTACLES*, reversed, which means family misfortune, loss of an inheritance, or caution against getting involved in a project that may be a poor risk. How can we fit these two together—the House and the card? Wendy is too young to be concerned with a profession, so it must be her mother we should think of. Perhaps, through the actions of her mother and brother, an inheritance that should come to Wendy will be diverted to them. Or they may refuse to let her use the money until she is older. But she needs it now in order to get away from the bickering at home and go to a more compatible school.

11. *AQUARIUS:* This House rules friends, groups, clubs; also hopes, wishes. *THE HIEROPHANT*, which fell here, suggests the need to conform and the importance of social approval. Perhaps Wendy, having already lost a friend, will now see the need of greater conformity to society.

This may be necessary for her to gain admittance to the new school.

12. *PISCES* stands for secret enemies, secret desires; also hidden limitations. *THE LOVERS* suggests that there is a choice confronting Wendy, a struggle within her own soul to find a balance in her life between her desire to be "somebody" and have a happy life, and, on the other hand (because she cannot please her mother), to run away and not finish school at all—something she may later regret.

From this reading, Wendy does not seem to have a very good chance of getting away from home and going to a boarding school. At the beginning of the chart, it looked as if the money would be found; later on, the trouble over an inheritance suggests that the money may be diverted or there may not be enough for the school, or that it must be found elsewhere. Therefore, she must learn balance in her emotions and try not to irritate her mother at every step—in other words, she must try to cooperate with her mother more than she has done thus far. If her tendency to wildness is curbed, she will get the approval of more mature people in the community, among whom she may find someone to help her realize her desires.

Lesson 17

SOLAR CHART METHOD
OF DIVINATION

This procedure is somewhat similar to the Horoscope method, but it is both more complete and a little more complicated. It is, nevertheless, worth learning, since it is most revealing in interpreting the character and problems of the Seeker.

In Astrology, when the time of birth is not known to the exact hour, the Seeker's Sun sign is sometimes placed on the cusp of the First House, known as the Ascendant. The chart thus erected is the Solar Chart. The following procedure is based on this chart. Each of the twelve signs of the Zodiac has been correlated with a Tarot card from the Major Arcana whose meaning is similar. These are given in detail in Lesson 15; an abbreviated list follows:

ARIES	March 21—April 19	The Sun, Key 19
TAURUS	April 20—May 20	The Hierophant, Key 5
GEMINI	May 21— June 20	The Lovers, Key 6
CANCER	June 21— July 22	Temperance, Key 14
LEO	July 23— Aug. 22	Strength, Key 8
VIRGO	Aug. 23— Sept. 22	The Hermit, Key 9
LIBRA	Sept. 23— Oct. 22	Justice, Key 11

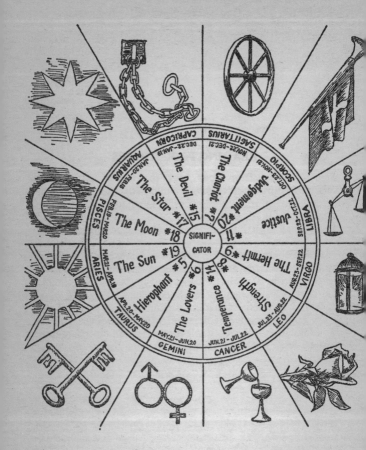

Diagram 3—The Solar Chart Method

SCORPIO	Oct.	22—Nov.	21	Judgement, Key 20
SAGITTARIUS	Nov.	22—Dec.	21	The Chariot, Key 7
CAPRICORN	Dec.	22—Jan.	19	The Devil, Key 15
AQUARIUS	Jan.	20—Feb.	18	The Star, Key 17
PISCES	Feb.	19—March	20	The Moon, Key 18

READING PROCEDURES

Step 1. Select from your pack the twelve Tarot cards mentioned above, and place them on the table in a large circle, starting with the Sun, Key 19, which is to be placed in the position of Aries, the First House, at the left and a little below center, as in Diagram 3. The remaining eleven cards are arranged in a circle with the Hierophant, Key 5, placed on Taurus, and so forth. By following Diagram 3, you can see exactly where to place each of these twelve special cards.

Step 2. Ask the Seeker which sign he was born under. Let us say, for example, that it was Gemini, the Lovers. Now slide the entire circle of cards around to the left slowly so that their positions are not disturbed, until you have the Lovers over the First House. Then Temperance will rest on Second House, Leo on Third House, and so on.

If the Seeker was born under the sign of Scorpio, Judgement, Key 20, then the circle of cards should be moved around until Judgement rests on the First House, the Chariot on the Second, the Devil on the Third. In this manner, one gets a different reading for each sign, but the same reading for all persons born under that sign. (At the end of this chapter are a two-part, movable Solar Chart Diagram and instructions for using it.)

Step 3. Read each card, starting with the one over the First House, and interpret the meaning of the card in conjunction with the affairs of the House. If you were reading for someone born under the sign of Gemini, you would correlate the meaning of the Lovers with those of Aries; the financial affairs of the Second House with

Temperance, and so on all around the Zodiac. This is the general reading for all people born under Gemini. To get an additional individualized reading, leave the twelve Major Arcana cards as they are for Gemini. Then:

Step 4. Ask the Seeker to shuffle the remaining cards and cut them as usual. The Reader now picks up the pack and turns up the top card, placing it on the First House, a little to the side of the card already there. The second card is turned up on the Second House, and so on through the Twelfth House. (The remaining cards are laid aside.)

Step 5. The specialized reading for the Seeker is now ready to be interpreted. It will be based on the general characteristics of the Seeker, as just read, but now combined with his own personality traits as seen in the second row of cards.

The reading must take into account the affairs of each House in relation to the general characteristics of the Seeker as shown by his birth sign, as well as the character analysis of that particular person as shown by the second row of cards. Here you will find that the cards often indicate present or future situations in the life of the Seeker, as well as indications about how someone with this type of personality can best handle these situations.

A READING BY THE SOLAR CHART METHOD

This reading was done for Lenore, a rather remarkable woman who seemed to be constantly beset by hard luck in both her personal life and career. Her birth sign is Aquarius, so we placed the Star on the First House, with the other special Arcana cards following after. The first card under each sign is the general reading for an Aquarian; the second card is from the cards shuffled and cut by Lenore herself, thus making the second card specifically applicable to her.

ARIES: *A.* THE STAR. Aquarians in general maintain a youthful and attractive appearance until well beyond their middle years. They radiate good health and an air of unselfish concern for others.

B. THE KING OF SWORDS. At the present time, a man in authority who is closely connected with Lenore will offer wise counsel, which should be taken.

TAURUS: *A.* THE MOON. The Aquarian does not always have a good sense for handling financial and material affairs. He will sometimes follow hunches that can lead to loss.

B. QUEEN OF CUPS. Lenore has had many dreams and projects concerned with financial gain, but they do not often materialize, and when they do the advantage is temporary. Thus, the Seeker is a typical Aquarian in money matters.

GEMINI: *A.* THE SUN. There are good relations with brothers and sisters, with many happy times together. The Aquarian may find fulfillment in writing that is connected with the arts and sciences.

B. EIGHT OF PENTACLES. The card of apprenticeship. Lenore is becoming skillful in matters of business and in handiwork. Writing could be included here, but the card would indicate she still has much to learn. Her relatives do not seem to come into the picture.

CANCER: *A.* THE HIEROPHANT. Aquarians often suffer from being in a family that is highly conventional and so places great importance on social approval. Since this is in direct opposition to the Aquarians' nature, which is unconventional and open to new ideas, they are often unhappy in their early home life.

B. TWO OF PENTACLES. Lenore is able to handle both the conventional and the unconventional and remain friends with all. She will come out unscathed from the changing ups and downs in her life.

LEO: *A.* THE LOVERS. The person under this sign has trouble making a choice between sacred and profane love.

B. THREE OF SWORDS. The Seeker has had or will have unhappy love affairs. The promise of a lasting relationship seems likely to be delayed for some time.

VIRGO: *A.* TEMPERANCE. The indication of good health shown in the First House by the Star is here reinforced. Aquarians make good coordinators and managers.

B. ACE OF WANDS. Lenore may shortly begin a new enterprise or project connected with health or food that has a fair chance of success.

LIBRA: *A.* STRENGTH. When an Aquarian marries, it is usually for idealistic reasons. The woman taming the lion here also suggests that in dealing with the public, the person under this sign can dominate, but at the same time use gentleness and tact.

B. SIX OF SWORDS. Lenore has moved away from an unhappy love affair (Three of Swords in the Fifth House), and will find her happiness after a journey, possibly by water.

SCORPIO: *A.* THE HERMIT. Aquarians have the ability to guide others; they make good counselors.

B. FIVE OF PENTACLES, reversed. Scorpio is the House of legacies, taxes, and the occult; somehow it must be fitted in with the spiritual meanings of the two cards. We must define this with the interpretation that Lenore is about to develop an interest in spiritual matters, which she may have neglected in the past.

SAGITTARIUS: *A.* JUSTICE. One of the outstanding traits of Aquarians is their ability to eliminate useless, outworn philosophies or religions from their life. When they believe in a concept, they have the ability to lead others forward into greater spiritual awareness.

B. SIX OF PENTACLES, reversed. This Aquarian trait has been stifled in Lenore by her overconcern with money and material problems. She must try to change her attitude so that her normal Aquarian gifts for leadership can function.

CAPRICORN: *A.* JUDGEMENT. The Aquarian is not concerned with worldly acclaim and honor. Perfected Aquarians are forerunners of the New Aquarian Age, and they are helping to bring about a change in mass consciousness.

B. TEN OF CUPS, reversed. The Seeker still has far to go. A loss of friendship is noted here. The betrayal may be from within her own nature.

AQUARIUS: *A.* THE CHARIOT. People born under this sign have the possibility of achieving greatness; they can influence friends and associates and help organizations in attaining purposeful programs.

B. EIGHT OF CUPS. Lenore may come to the point of dropping her present situation of bondage to material problems and can, if she wishes, realize her true Aquarian powers.

PISCES: *A.* THE DEVIL. The unrealized Aquarian may struggle all his life to free himself from bondage to the material. This is his own personal struggle, and no one else can give much help. This is his secret enemy.

B. SEVEN OF SWORDS. Lenore finds that her efforts toward self-realization are only partially successful. The advice to be given here is that she rally all her potential powers and strive mightily to realize the wonder that lies waiting in the stars.

Summary

Lenore has had a great many problems, and she is still trying to find her rightful place. She is hindered by insufficient money and poor job situations. There is a tendency here to value money too highly, probably because it has loomed up as an obstacle in her life. Some of her relationships, particularly with men, turn out badly. She has great unused and unrealized potential, and could be a leading force in a movement toward some better form of society, but her inner struggle and insecurity about this potential hold her back for the present.

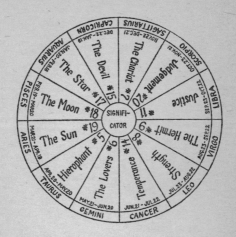

Diagram 4A—Solar Chart

DIRECTIONS FOR USING THE SOLAR CHART CUTOUT

On this page and page 191 is the two-part Solar Chart diagram mentioned earlier, which is especially designed to help students in using the Solar Chart method. Cut out the round "wheel" (Diagram 4A) and position it in the blank circle in Diagram 4B. A pin will help to hold the "wheel" in position while it is being turned to align the birth sign of the Seeker with the First House. Another reading is given using this movable Solar Chart in Additional Tarot Readings at the end of the book.

Diagram 4B—Solar Chart

Lesson 18

THE USE AND MISUSE
OF THE TAROT

I have left this very important subject to the last, since I feel that now, after you have gained an understanding of the cards, you will more readily comprehend how serious a misuse of the cards may be and how conscientious you must be with your new knowledge.

Only a few days ago I received the following letter from a young woman of twenty who is currently attending a small eastern college:

"It is now several months since an amateur palmist revealed a terrible future in my hands. This disturbed me so much that my family and friends have become concerned about the change in me. My future, as she read it, was as follows: I would lack the qualities I needed to pursue a career; my life would be a succession of routine jobs; I would have two marriages—both disastrous; my life would come to an end in middle age."

Needless to say, I was greatly upset by her letter; she was obviously very deeply affected by what the amateur palmist had predicted. I hastened to assure her that neither palmistry, Astrology, the Tarot, nor any other occult discipline could possibly predict anything of the future with precise accuracy. Her amateur palmist had been most irresponsible, and it would be wise for her to toss the "predictions" out the window. I told her that each of us makes his destiny, and that she could become anything she really wanted to and could have a life of her own making.

A week later I received her reply. She wrote: "The dread of a negative response from you was almost overwhelming, to the point of my nearly leaving your answer unread. Thank God I didn't! Your words were like capsules of dynamite, exploding old fantasies as well as old fears, and yet I was not left feeling futile but rather uplifted. There was no better answer to be had for me, Dr. Gray, for even a good Tarot reading could not have conquered the alienation I was experiencing between me and myself—and God." (She had asked me to do a reading for her but I had refused, feeling that she was in too susceptible and apprehensive a state.)

I remember, too, the experience of a friend who, in her early years, had lived in St. Louis. One rainy Sunday she and another young girl had found an old pack of Tarot cards in a drawer and spread them out on the floor. My young friend, at random—for she did not know the meanings of the cards—tried to read the other girl's fortune. The pseudo-fortune-teller later moved to New York, and after some years revisited St. Louis and telephoned her old chum. To her astonishment, the other girl burst into recriminations, accusing my friend of having created a chronic nervous condition in her by predicting awful things in her future that rainy Sunday when she had carelessly played at being a soothsayer. No amount of explanation or expressions of regret could change the woman's mind; she was convinced she had suffered irreparable damage. From that time on, my friend shied away from any form of divination—she realized how powerful a suggestion could be, especially a negative one.

There are numerous young people in college and high school today who are finding it fun to delve into the occult. Many of them, even in this age of science and reason, seem to be very gullible and superstitious, ready to believe the best or the worst on the turn of a card or a star. They would probably laugh if someone crossed himself for luck or refused to walk under a ladder, but there they are, turning their bright young lives into times of torture as they wait for a dire assortment of evil things to happen to them.

The Tarot for centuries was used for fortune-telling, while hidden in its symbolism was the highest philosophy, the eternal religion that shows man as emanating from the Divine and points out the path he must ascend in order to realize consciously the truth of his being—that he himself is Divine.

The cards of the Major Arcana, particularly, express these thoughts in picture form. For example, the Chariot, Key 7, warns us to beware of being purely intellectual, for the charioteer who controls his passions only by the use of his mind and will, at any moment that he loses his control can be split asunder. Think of the woman taming the lion in Key 8. This represents the passions she has under control—whether they are sexual feelings or the passion for conquest. She, unlike the charioteer, uses spiritual force and by this method easily closes the lion's mouth. Several cards give the lesson of balance by depicting a figure seated between the columns of the negative and positive. The Moon card shows the dangers that may lurk in the psychic or the occult, indicating how carefully one must walk, keeping to the middle of the path. The Hanged Man has reversed his life completely, and depends on the guidance of Spirit alone.

The first four cards of the Major Arcana tell of man's creative ability and how he can turn his thoughts and ideas into concrete form. The Magician symbolizes the mind of man in its potentiality; with his magic wand of the will he can create all things, whether they be under the influence of the red roses of desire or the white lilies of spiritual thought. The High Priestess is the subconscious mind, that great unknown realm where all creation takes place. We all have a great store of ideas in our conscious minds, and we also have a subconscious which, without questioning whether these ideas are right or wrong, accepts them and proceeds to carry them out.

If we do not deliberately fill the subconscious with creative, positive ideas, it will pick up and create destructively, according to our conscious thoughts, whether of danger, fear, or just plain acceptance of the prevailing negative world-thought around us.

The Emperor represents controlled thought, the realm of reason, that can impregnate the subconscious with the ideas it wants to see manifested in the outer realm; the Empress shows us the delightful, happy fruitfulness that results from the right penetration of that ever-willing, ever-creative subconscious. One might say that the motto of the subconscious mind is "Ours not to question why, ours but to do or die."

In reading the Tarot cards for ourselves or others, if we take a negative interpretation too literally, we are putting negative ideas down into the subconscious by way of the emotions. Fear and worry are emotions, and when they are not governed by reason they reproduce in our lives the very things we fear.

This is the wisdom of the Tarot; interpretations may vary, but at the core its philosophy remains to guide us in every walk of life and in every situation.

But, along with this guidance, ask this question of yourself: "What is my concept of myself?" And, "How was it formed?" The answer is: "Out of past experience and what others have said or thought about me, good or bad." We act the way we do because of our concept or conviction of who and what we are. When we change this concept, we act differently. A changed concept automatically alters our future. What we assume will be our experience becomes our experience, for assumptions passed on to the subconscious are acted upon, and we see the results around us.

All outer change first takes place in consciousness—we cannot repeat that too often. At every moment of our lives, we have before us a choice of actions. Will we get up or remain seated? Will we finish that task now or wait till tomorrow? Will we go to college in Denver or Miami? Will we study or fool away our days? If we assume we will have a negative future because of a reading, this assumption brings forth the very future we do not want.

Once upon a time, in a kingdom far away, a young prince was stolen by the Gypsies and brought up to believe he was one of them. He lived their life, went hungry, and danced and sang before their campfires. After many years the king and his courtiers, hunting in the forest, came upon a young lad asleep under a tree.

Looking at him closely, the king noticed a birthmark that identified the lad positively as his long-lost son, and the heir to the throne. The lad was told who he was, to his astonishment, and was brought to the castle, where he was given fine clothes, a suite of rooms, and servitors. He had assumed for so long that he was a Gypsy that he found it hard to accept his rightful position. At banquets he would take food from the table to hide under his pillow, in case this strange dream vanished and he found himself hungry again. When, at last, he could change his concept of himself, he was able to accept his new position as prince of the realm.

Most of us act as though we were brought up by the Gypsies. We feel that the wonderful things of life are for others, not for us—we are too tall, too fat, too short, not well-coordinated, not very bright; our parents were too rich or too poor, too permissive or too strict; it was our brothers and sisters who got all the attention—and so on. What keeps you from being all you would like to be?

The truth is we are all princes and princesses of the realm; we have all been given the power to choose. Do you choose to live a wonderful life full of adventure and excitement? Assume you have it NOW, and your subconscious will reproduce it for you. Assume the opposite sex finds you attractive, and it will. All change takes place first in consciousness, so assume you are moving forward on the path you have chosen, and events will follow the assumption. The Tarot, when it is properly read and interpreted, can help you realize your greatest ambitions.

> "Man is not a creature of circumstances,
> Circumstances are the creatures of men."
> —Disraeli

So watch for the pitfalls when you read the cards; recognize how very suggestible everyone is—and then go ahead and use the cards for good. You have been warned sufficiently about hasty and negative interpretations of your precious Tarot cards. Give those for whom you read encouragement to strive for their highest ideals.

THE SEEDS YOU PLANT CAN BLOSSOM INTO LOVELY FLOWERS OF ACCOMPLISHMENT.

ADDITIONAL TAROT READINGS

One of the most difficult things for the beginning student of the Tarot is to be able to make a running story after he has laid out the cards in a spread. He knows the meanings of each card, or looks them up to refresh his memory, but he has trouble making a connected story out of them. The Seeker has asked a question of the cards silently or aloud. (At the beginning of the Reader's experience, the question had better be asked out loud as a guide to his interpretation; later on, he can let the Seeker ask the question of the Tarot silently.) Before them lie the cards that have come up in answer, cards for the past, the present, and the future, for people and for situations, and now they must be coordinated into a general picture, a running story that pertains to the question. The following readings, along with their interpretations, are given here as an added help.

READING 1 (KELTIC METHOD)

Question: Will Alice, a mature woman, remarry?

In choosing a Significator I could not be guided by Alice's white hair, so I chose the Queen of Cups for her as I knew she had written poetry and composed the words and music of some songs. Alice is a widow, with no children, and is working part-time. The man who has asked her to marry him is a widower who lives with his grown son in a suburb. This is the way the cards fell:

1. *Four of Swords, reversed:* Among the meanings of this card are renewed activity, caution to use discretion in all

one's dealings. Other meanings are social unrest and labor strikes. Naturally, the last two meanings would not apply to Alice's question, so we will use the first two. I told her that this new man in her life would certainly cause renewed activity, and that as an older woman she definitely should use caution in making the decision to remarry.

2. *Eight of Wands,* meaning approach to goal, arrows of love, haste, hope. I showed her how each of these would fit into her present situation and told her that therefore this second card, rather than being in opposition to the first, would go along with it.

3. *Justice:* For this card I chose the meaning: beginning of a new cycle in Alice's life, with the possibility of a good balance between business and home life. Since Justice was positioned in the past, I asked Alice if she had not been lonely a good part of the time, with her job taking most of her attention. She nodded in agreement, saying she had wanted a better, balanced life and that now that this man was taking her out a good deal, she had already begun to experience the type of life she desired.

4. *The Magician:* The Magician is a creator, a builder. This card was in the position of what was now becoming a thing of the past. When I explained this to Alice, she admitted that she had been creating in her imagination the sort of freer life she would like to lead. I showed her that as things now stood, she no longer needed to create for the future, but could live it in the present.

5. *The Hierophant, reversed:* No. 5 is the position of what *may* happen in the future, and the card's meanings are unconventionality, openness to new ideas. I asked Alice if there was the possibility of their living together without getting married. "No," Alice said, "that idea has not come up, but marrying a man a good deal younger than myself seems unconventional enough."

6. *The Chariot, reversed:* This card means sudden collapse of a project, ill health, a journey postponed. Being in the position of the future, the Chariot did not augur well for the marriage. I suggested to Alice the possibility that one

or the other of them might become ill, not seriously, but enough to postpone the marriage. And that instead of a journey, the card could mean a change of residence delayed. She told me that, when they got married, she planned to give up her little apartment in the city and move into his house in the suburb.

7. *Judgement:* Awakening, change of position, renewed energy and health. This card was in the position of Alice's fears. Did she fear a change of position or status? Could she cope with cooking and with a grown stepson in the house? She admitted that these worries had crossed her mind. She had feared that her health, though good, could not stand up to the new demands that would be made upon her, and she recognized that the man's son had been spoiled and was inconsiderate and selfish.

8. *Temperance, reversed:* Have you noticed that there are six cards of the Major Arcana in this spread? This would mean that other strong influences were at work here over which Alice had no control. The meanings of Temperance, reversed, are bad management, unfortunate combinations, competing interests, lack of good judgment. The No. 8 position refers to what those around the pair think of the marriage. I asked Alice what kind of reactions they had had. She told me that several of their mutual friends wondered if it would work out, and that the son seemed jealous of the time her suitor spent with her. "Yes," I said, "that is what the card seems to indicate."

9. *The Ten of Cups* fell here in the position of Alice's hopes; here was the epitome of her wish for a truly happy married life. When I told her this, she shyly admitted that this was indeed her desire.

10. *King of Wands,* a blond man of enterprise. I asked Alice if this card could possibly represent the man she was engaged to, a man of enterprise and authority. She said, "Yes"; that he was rather blond, the head of his department in business, and well looked up to. This card can also betoken a good marriage. As it was the last card, that of the final outcome, I told her that in spite of drawbacks it looked as if the marriage would eventually take place.

The Major Arcana in the spread indicated that the other influences might delay matters somewhat—and the King of Wands, being the last card, indicated that it would be up to this man to make the final arrangements and set the date.

The question, will Alice, a mature woman, remarry? seemed to have been answered by the Tarot with a definite Yes, in spite of her secret fears and the possibility of delay.

READING 2 (KELTIC METHOD)

This question, asked in the spring of 1971, has to do with a matter none of us can answer with certainty until the fall of 1972. I asked: Will President Nixon win the next presidential election?

For President Nixon's Significator, I chose the King of Swords.

1. *Ace of Wands:* Here is the question in its entirety, for the Ace of Wands covers him, indicating the general atmosphere that surrounds the question. The card means "the beginning of an enterprise, the beginning of a family or a fortune," and here the beginning specifically refers to the beginning of another four years in the White House.

2. *The Hierophant:* The opposing forces for good or evil. This would indicate that Nixon, doing all the things he considered right and best for the country, still showed no evidence of spiritual inspiration or guidance.

3. *The Emperor:* This is the basis of the matter in relation to what has occurred in the past. Here we have kingship, leadership in government, control over the masses, and war-making power. Certainly Nixon has shown leadership, and he has proved that he has war-making power.

4. *Five of Wands:* This is an influence that is passing away. The meanings of this card are quarreling, competition, strife, and the battle of life. Nixon has put up a good fight, but the opposition has been strong, with much quarreling and strife over his policies.

5. *Page of Wands, reversed:* This position represents an event that may happen in the future. The Five of Wands, reversed, shows that disputes continue, that there may be trickery involved somewhere. The general public may often not be given the truth about the war in Vietnam. There will be even more heated disputes over the way the country is governed.

6. *The Hanged Man, reversed:* This card is in the position of the future, suggesting what will come to pass. The card reflects absorption in physical matters, preoccupation with power, possibly false prophecies. Will Nixon become arrogant and preoccupied with his political image? This is a suggestion of false prophecy, but by whom?

7. *Wheel of Fortune, reversed:* This represents fears, and would seem to refer to the President's fear of failure. In any case, he will reap what he has sown.

8. *Justice, reversed:* This is what those around the candidate think of his chances for a second term. They feel he has dealt too severely with his opponents, but still they do not wish to judge him too harshly. (The Hanged Man near this card indicates that he should be leniently judged.)

9. *Seven of Pentacles:* This is the card of Nixon's hopes in the matter. He feels he has grown during his years in the White House, and tends to believe that any unfavorable reactions to him are only temporary and will pass away by election time.

10. *Four of Pentacles, reversed:* This is the position of the final result. The country feels he has been unwise with the resources and money of the nation. There will be setbacks in material aspirations, and this seems to indicate that he will lose the election. The card also conveys the possibility that there will be a loss of earthly possessions. This may well mean the loss of the White House, his presidential salary, and all the perquisites of office. The card also indicates opposition, which, obviously, came from all those who opposed his reelection.

The final answer to the question posed the Tarot is as I have summarized in step No. 10. It would be ill advised to make any bets on this prediction, for there are many factors that could change in the time that remains. This reading is an example of how the student can take a national or international question and read the cards for it.

SAMPLE READING 3 (SOLAR CHART METHOD)

This reading was for Betsy, born under the sign of Cancer. She asked no specific question, wanting to know simply how things stood for her at the present time. Using your two-part solar chart, place Cancer-Temperance on the First House by putting the small wheel inside the blank circle on the rectangular part of the chart. See how easily, then, you can get a reading for all Cancerians.

    A. Character analysis for all persons born under the sign of Cancer.

    B. The working out of the present situation for the person you are reading for—in this case, Betsy.

ARIES: *A.* TEMPERANCE, the card equated with Cancer, rests here. The Cancerian's personality is well balanced and well coordinated.

    B. KING OF WANDS, reversed. This man, strict in his judgments, is closely associated with Betsy, and his influence is affecting her basic personality.

TAURUS: *A.* STRENGTH on Taurus makes the Cancerian likely to use money wisely and with strength of purpose.

    B. THE FOOL, Key 12, fell here. At the present time Betsy has an important choice to make with regard to her financial affairs. She should be careful to use her Cancerian power wisely in making her choice.

GEMINI: *A.* THE HERMIT. A Cancerian is a thoughtful person, not given to rash actions or statements. He may be interested in writing on spiritual matters or have a brother or sister who does writing of this sort.

    B. FOUR OF SWORDS. Note that a card, one of whose meanings is "hermit's repose," falls on the Hermit card. As the meanings of these cards coincide, it means that

Betsy should be doubly sure at this time to seek rest and solitude away from relatives, and await a change for the better.

CANCER: *A.* JUSTICE. The Cancerian often has a good early home life, with the accent on education. By maturity, Cancerians have achieved a well-rounded personality and some recognition for work done in science, chemistry, or cooking.

B. QUEEN OF WANDS. A blonde woman, sound in her business judgments, will be interested in Betsy and help her to achieve success.

LEO: *A.* JUDGEMENT. This card means awakening, renewal. The Cancerian may possibly have had faulty judgment in the past in regard to a love affair or speculation. But an awakening occurs sometime in his life and he becomes a better-balanced personality.

B. FIVE OF CUPS, reversed. This would seem to indicate that in the case of Betsy the awakening will be coming shortly and may be caused by another person, or experienced in the company of another, possibly an old friend.

VIRGO: *A.* THE CHARIOT. It is very important for a Cancerian to eat a well-balanced diet and to avoid overindulgence in food or drink. The Chariot indicates that his care of his health will depend on a strong will, enough strength of character to control the indulgence of his desires. These people do very well at artistic work, though this is not necessarily their profession.

B. KING OF CUPS, reversed. This card is reversed, so Betsy should watch for this man who is connected with the arts or Betsy's art work. He can be both violent and crafty, and could cause her loss or scandal, or both.

LIBRA: *A.* THE DEVIL. The Cancerian is likely to be unduly attracted by money and good looks when planning a marriage or a partnership. He should be on guard against anyone who seems to be trying to place him in a position of bondage.

B. SEVEN OF CUPS, reversed, fell here. It shows that Betsy has the determination and will power to enable her to keep from coming under anyone else's control. A happy marriage is more possible for this Cancerian than for the average.

SCORPIO: *A.* THE STAR. The Cancerian is not one who waits impatiently for a legacy. He usually cultivates a healthy attitude toward the possibility of a future inheritance.

B. KNIGHT OF CUPS fell here, which would indicate that there is a young man who, when the time comes, will be of great help to Betsy in matters of taxes and inheritance.

SAGITTARIUS: *A.* THE MOON. Cancerians operate from the subconscious and emotional level rather than the intellect when forming their philosophies and ideals. But they should be careful not to delve too deeply into psychic fields.

B. NINE OF SWORDS. This may indicate a rather bad time for Betsy if she does become involved with psychic issues—or even too much with her own imagination. It might cause an illness or breakdown. Long journeys should be put off. The advice given in the Third House for Betsy is here repeated more forcefully, and should be heeded.

CAPRICORN: *A.* THE SUN. The Cancerian can attain material happiness and success, perhaps some public acclaim, probably through the arts or sciences. He takes pleasure in the simple life and even refrains from accepting the honors he deserves.

B. NINE OF CUPS. This is the wish card, and such a promising one that it reaffirms for Betsy the success predicted above.

AQUARIUS: *A.* THE HIEROPHANT. A Cancerian is likely to choose his friends and associates from the conventional walks of life. He may put too much emphasis on social approval and conformity. He may go to church for the music instead of looking for spiritual inspiration.

B. QUEEN OF CUPS, reversed. Note that in this reading we have had two Kings reversed, and now a Queen. This would seem to indicate that Betsy draws to herself a number of people who do not promote her best interests. Here the Queen of Cups is a woman with light brown hair and hazel eyes. Under her conventional appearance, she may be immoral as well as dishonest.

PISCES: *A.* THE LOVERS. There is a chance here of self-undoing for the Cancerian. Perhaps in choosing a marriage or a business partner (the Devil in the Seventh House), or friends (the Hierophant in the Eleventh House), the Cancerian reacts too much to their outer physical attraction. As the Cancerian's true nature (Temperance in the First House) is one of balance and harmony, these two aspects of their lives may cause great inner conflict.

B. EIGHT OF CUPS. The solution for Betsy, it would seem, is the same one as that pointed out previously in the Third House. When things get rough, Betsy should endeavor to take a solitary vacation and, through much self-searching, find a harmonious solution to her major problem.

Summary

Others play an important role in Betsy's life at the present time; some work for her best interests (Queen of Wands, Knight of Cups), but others should be avoided when possible (King of Wands, reversed), King of Cups, reversed, and Queen of Cups, reversed. Betsy should seek to make her decisions and solve her problems through solitary contemplation and reflection. After this, the balanced solution will come. But she must shun psychic or occult involvement. Eventual success in work and money matters seems assured, but she must use her own innate powers to bring this about.

READING 4 (KELTIC METHOD)

Captain K. was just back from three years in Indochina and had seen some fighting in Vietnam. He was in town with his wife and small son, visiting his parents. He had seen enough service so that he could now retire from the army if he wished, or he could reenlist. Since his return, he had learned that at the present time many highly skilled men were out of work. His question to the Tarot was: Should I stay in the service, or should I leave the army and seek civilian employment?

I chose the King of Swords as Captain K.'s Significator because of its warlike qualities and not because of his hair coloring.

Here is the way the cards fell for him:

1. *Three of Pentacles,* meaning skill and mastery. The first position represents the atmosphere surrounding his question; it obviously had to do with his finding employment. This first card showed me that the Tarot was "on the beam" and that the reading would be a clear and satisfactory one.

2. *Queen of Swords,* in the position of opposing forces. As Captain K. was the King of Swords, this Queen must represent his wife. I said to him, "Your wife is against your reenlistment." "Yes," he replied, "she is very much against it. She wants me to stay home now that she's got me back."

3. *The Sun:* I explained to Captain K. that this card had fallen on the position that was the basis of the matter, and that the Sun meant attainment, a good marriage, and pleasure in the simple life. "This is what you want really, isn't it?" He nodded.

4. *Page of Pentacles, reversed,* means that the Seeker is surrounded by people whose ideas are in opposition to his own. I pointed out to him that this card indicated not only was his wife against his reenlistment, but his parents were, too.

5. *Four of Swords, reversed:* This card had fallen on the position that indicates what may happen in the future. I told him that, in the reversed position, it cautioned him to use discretion and to remember the necessary economies in making his final decision.

6. *Seven of Wands:* Here in the position of the future, I told him, the card suggested there would be stiff competi-

tion whether he decided on a business career or sought promotion in the army.

7. *Seven of Pentacles, reversed:* I explained to Captain K. that this card was in the position of his fears. I asked him if he was worried about money matters, and he admitted that he was. The card also suggested, I pointed out, that there was likely to be a time interval before more money came in, and he had better be careful of what he had.

8. *The Seven of Cups* represented what his family and those around him thought about his problem. I said, "They see you pulled both ways. Also, the card indicates that you have a great many conflicting plans and desires, and nothing much can happen for you until you decide for yourself what you really want to do."

9. *The Ten of Cups* was in the position of his hopes. I pointed out to Captain K. that he hoped, above all, for a happy family life, perhaps another child; and that there were two in the card, and enough success to own a moderate-priced home.

10. *Six of Swords:* This card shows a woman and child being poled across troubled waters to a farther shore. No. 10 is the final card, the one on which rest the findings of all the others. I told Captain K. that it looked as if his wife and son would take a journey over water. Did that mean anything to him? He said, "Yes," that if he reenlisted he probably would not be sent to Indochina again, but to some place like Europe, where he could have his family with him.

I told him the Tarot indicated that he would be much too unsure of himself, at the present time, in civilian life, and that despite both his wife's and his parents' wishes, he would try another "hitch" in the army. He would most probably be happier in the environment that he already knew. As to whether he *should* or not, the Tarot rarely replies *should* to a question, but rather points out both sides of the problem, leaving the final choice always up to the Seeker.

GLOSSARY

ANGEL—1. *Raphael*, angel of air. Symbol of the superconscious (Key 6). 2. *Michael*, angel of fire and sun (Key 14). 3. *Gabriel*, angel of water (Key 20).

ANKH—Egyptian symbol of life, generation; combines the masculine and feminine (Key 4).

ANUBIS—Jackal-headed Egyptian god representing the evolution of consciousness from lower to higher levels. Also the Egyptian equivalent of Hermes or Mercury, signifying self-consciousness, intellectuality (Key 10).

BANNER (Also STANDARD or FLAG)—Betokens freedom from material bonds; action, vibration. Carried in the left hand, it indicates that control of vibration has passed from the right hand (self-consciousness) to the left (subconsciousness) and has become automatic. (Keys 10, 13, 19, 20).

BULL—Sign of Taurus in Astrology. Assigned to the suit of Pentacles to indicate they are of the element earth.

BUTTERFLY—Symbol of the immortality of the soul and of the element air. Knight, Queen, and King of Swords show butterflies in the designs of their cards.

CAT—A black cat indicates the sinister aspect of Venus.

CHAIN—Restriction, largely self-imposed.

CIRCLE—Eternity, spirit.

CRESCENT—Soul.

CROSS—Solar cross has equal arms to indicate the union of the male, positive element (upright), with the female, negative element (horizontal), or the union with God and earth. (Keys 2, 20).

CROWN—Attainment, mastery. The Will, which may be set against the cosmic purpose. Represents the creative, formative, and material world. (Keys 3, 5, 16).

CUBE—Sometimes a square. Represents earth, material manifestation. Order and measurement. That which was, is, and shall be. (Key 15).

CUPS—Associated with the concept of water (see suit of Cups, Minor Arcana). The cup is a symbol of knowledge and preservation. It also means love, pleasure, and enjoyment. (Key 14).

CYPRESS TREE—Sacred to Venus (Key 3 and Court cards of Swords).

DEVIL—Symbolizes the false conception that man is bound by material conditions, that he is a slave to necessity and blind chance. The Devil is sensation divorced from understanding by spiritual blindness. (Key 15).

DOG—Friend, helper, and companion to man. Indicates that all nonhuman forms of life are elevated and improved by the advance of human consciousness. (Keys 0, 18).

DOVE—Descent of Spirit, peace.

EAGLE—One of the symbols denoting the four seasons or the four suits of the Minor Arcana. The Eagle is associated with Scorpio (the Scorpion), the eighth sign of the Zodiac. It is a symbol of power. (Keys 10, 21).

EARTH—Symbol of concrete physical manifestations (Keys 14, 17).

ELLIPSE—The superconscious (Key 21).

FIGURE EIGHT ON ITS SIDE—Eternal life, the cosmic lemniscate. Harmonious interaction between the conscious and the subconscious, between life and feeling, desire and emotion. May mean dominion over the material. (Keys 1, 8).

FISH—Idea or thought. In the King of Cups the fish is seen coming from the sea of the universal subconscious. In the Page of Cups it is arising from his own subconscious.

FLAME—Spirit.

FLOWERS—White flowers: spiritual thoughts, love, happiness. Red flowers: human desires.

FRUIT—Fertility.

GLOBE—(See Orb of the World.) Symbol of dominion (Key 4).

GNOMES—Elements who live beneath the surface of the earth. Associated with the suit of Pentacles.

GOAT—Fertility, as when depicted on the arms of the throne of the Queen of Pentacles. Suggests bestiality and overindulgence in sex, as in Key 15, the Devil.

GOLD—Metal of the sun.

GRAPES—Abundance, pleasure. GRAPEVINES: a continuation and growth in abundance and pleasure.

HAND—Right hand, positive, masculine; left hand, negative, feminine.

HEART—Symbols in the shape of a heart refer to the subconscious, the emotions. (Key 3).

HORSE—Symbol of solar energy, or the controlled, subdued Life-force. (Keys 13, 19).

IHVH—Ancient Hebrew initials of the name Jehovah: I—Fire; H—Water; V—Air; H—Earth (Key 10).

IRIS—Represents Iris, Greek goddess of the rainbow, as in Key 14.

KEYS CROSSED—The Hidden Doctrine. One is of silver, the other gold—representing solar and lunar currents in radiant energy. (Key 5).

LAMP—Spiritual light, intelligence.

LEAVES—Growth, vitality.

LIGHT—Spiritual emanations, activity of God, life.

LIGHTNING—A flash of inspiration. The Life-power that descends down the Kabalistic Tree of Life.

LILY—Abstract thought untinged by desire (Key 1).

LION—King of the beasts; zodiacal sign Leo. Represents all-powerful subhuman force. May also stand for Mars (war). (Keys 8, 10, 21).

MIRROR OF VENUS—A solar cross surmounted by a circle; symbol of the planet Venus; indicates fertility. (Key 4).

MOON—A feminine astrological symbol of personality, also of the subconscious mind. The reflected light of the subconscious. (Keys 2, 18).

MOUNTAINS (SNOW-CAPPED PEAKS)—Indicate the cold, abstract principles of mathematics behind and above all warm, colorful, and vital activities of cosmic manifestation. Heights of abstract thought. Wisdom and understanding. (Keys 0, 6, 9, 14, 20).

ORB OF THE WORLD—A traditional symbol of the earth dominated by the Lord or the Spirit. (Key 4).

PALM—Symbol of victory over death, and of the male aspect of life. The active force, as shown on the veil behind the High Priestess. (Key 2).

PATH—The way to spiritual attainment and esoteric knowledge, as set forth in the Tarot cards (Keys 14, 18).

PENTACLE—The pentagram in the form of an amulet, believed to protect against evil spirits. (See suit of Pentacles, also Key 15).

PENTAGRAM (SEAL OF SOLOMON)—Five-pointed star, expressing mind's domination over the elements. Symbol of the Word made Flesh. Depending on the direction of its points, it may represent order or confusion. (Note that the pentagrams are right side up in the suit of Pentacles, reversed in Key 15).

PILLAR—1. *White Pillar* (Jachin) establishes the principle inherent in all things; the positive aspect of life; light. 2. *Black Pillar* (Boaz). Negation of activity, inertia; darkness (Keys 2, 5, 11)

POMEGRANATES—Symbol of the female, passive aspect of life; fecundity (Key 2).

PYRAMID—The earth in its maternal aspect. The triangular-shaped face of the pyramid suggests the threefold principle of creation.

RABBIT—Symbol of fertility.

RAINBOW—A Sign from God of future protection and happiness.

RAM'S HEAD—Symbol of Mars, war; power, leadership. Also First Sign of the Zodiac (Aries, the Ram). (Key 4).

ROSE—1. *White Rose:* Freedom from lower forms of desire and passion. 2. *Red Rose:* Represents Venus, nature, desire. Both are cultivated flowers, representing cultural activities. (Keys 0, 1).

SALAMANDER—Lizardlike creature able to live in the midst of fire. The elemental of the suit of Wands; also used in the Court cards.

SCALES—Balanced judgment (Key 11).

SCROLL—The Divine Law, the Hidden Mysteries. Past events impressed upon the subconscious. (Key 2).

SERPENT—Symbol of wisdom, for it tempts man to knowledge of himself. Secrecy, subtlety. Serpent biting its tail represents law of endless transformation; also represents radiant energy descending into manifestation. (Keys 1, 6, 10).

SHELLFISH—The early stages of conscious unfoldment. Related to the Zodiacal Sign of the Crab. May invade the territory of the waking consciousness and give rise to fears. (Key 18).

SHIP—Material treasure.

SILVER—Metal of the moon.

SPHINX—Symbol of the combination of human and animal attributes. The white sphinx betokens mercy; the black one, severity. Sometimes the Sphinx represents the human senses, which are continually propounding riddles. (Keys 7, 10).

SQUARE—Foursquare, the solidity of earth.

STAFF—Implement of the Magician; emblem of power.

STAR—Suggests Sixth Sign of the Zodiac. The six-pointed star (hexagram) indicates dominion over laws of the great world; the eight-pointed star represents cosmic order, radiant energy. (Keys 9, 17).

STONE—*Abn* is the Hebrew word for stone. *Aba*, stemming from the first two letters of the alphabet, means "father" (as in ABraham); *Bn* means "son" (*cf.* Ben-Gurion, son of Gurion). Thus, stone symbolizes the union of father and son, spirit and body; the Divine Wisdom and the human intellect. "Upon this rock [stone] will I build my church" (on the understanding that the Father and the Son are one). David slew Goliath with a stone, and with this understanding we can all slay the Goliaths in our lives.

STREAM—Symbolizes the stuff of life, forever flowing to the ocean of cosmic consciousness.

SUN—Source of light, dynamo of radiant energy whence all creatures derive their personal force (Keys 0, 6, 13, 19).

SUNFLOWERS—Nature in its fullness (Key 19).

SWORDS—Represent activity, either destructive or constructive (*see* suit of Swords). They also represent the rigors of the law; can mean the elimination of outworn forms. (Key 11).

SYLPH—An elemental of the air somewhat similar to a cupid. Associated with the suit of Swords.

TOWER—Represents a man's creation or personality, sometimes built on a foundation of false science. Misapprehension; the fallacy of personal isolation. (Keys 13, 16, 18).

TREE—1. *Tree of Knowledge of Good and Evil*, bearing five fruits, representing the five senses (in Key 6, it is seen behind Eve). 2. *Tree of Life*, bearing 12 fruits, representing the 12 signs of the Zodiac (Key 6, behind Adam).
Note: Under the appellations of the Tree of Life and the Tree of the Knowledge of Good and Evil is concealed the great arcanum of antiquity—the mystery of equilibrium. The Tree of Life represents the spiritual point of balance—the secret of immortality. The Tree of the Knowledge of Good and Evil represents polarity or imbalance—the secret of mortality. Though humanity is still wandering in the world of good and evil, it will ultimately attain completion and eat of the fruit of the Tree of Life growing in the midst of the illusionary garden of worldly things.

UNDINE—An elemental that lives in the water and is thus associated with the suit of Cups. Undines appear on the throne of the Queen of Cups.

VEIL—Indicates hidden things or ideas. Symbol of virginity. Only when the veil is rent or penetrated by concentrated impulses on self-conscious levels are the creative activities of the subconscious realized and actualized. (Keys 2, 11).

WAND—Symbol of Will and power. Suggests continual renewal of life. May have phallic significance. (*See* suit of Wands, also Key 21).

WATER—Symbolizes the subconscious, the emotions. Water in a pool symbolizes the reservoir of cosmic mind stuff, which can be stirred into vibration by the act of meditation. (Keys 14, 17, 18, 20).

WATER LILIES—Eternal life.

WHEAT—Abundance and fertility. Sacred to Hathor-Isis and all Mother goddesses. (Key 3).

WHEEL—Symbol of the whole cycle of cosmic expression. The center or pivot is the archetypal or thought world; the inner circle, creative; middle circle, formative; and the outer circle, the material world. The eight spokes, like the eight-pointed star, represent the channels of universal radiant energy. (Keys 7, 10).

WOLF—Symbolizes the manifestations of Nature before man has tamed and civilized them. (Key 18).

WREATH—Represents the forces of Nature, the kingdom of growing things. (Keys 3, 8, 21).

YOD (DROPS OF LIGHT)—Yod is the Hebrew letter symbolizing the hands of man. It betokens power, skill, dexterity. The descent of the Life-force from above into the conditions of material existence. Corresponds to the zodiacal sign of the Virgin. (Keys 16, 18).

ZERO—Symbol of the absence of quality, quantity, and mass. Denotes absolute freedom from every limitation. Sign of the infinite and eternal conscious energy. Superconsciousness. (Key 0).

ZODIAC—Symbol of cycle of existence.

INDEX

217

NOTE: Queries on the Tarot may be sent to the author at P.O. Box 3293, Vero Beach, Florida 32960.

Ⓞ SIGNET BOOKS

STRETCH THE LIMITS OF YOUR MIND

(0451)

☐ **YOUR MYSTERIOUS POWERS OF ESP by Harold Sherman.** Discover how your own extrasensory powers are just waiting for activation and development with this knowledgeable guide that will lead you to new forms of creativity, new forms of healing, new forms of enlightenment, awareness, and more! (093151—$1.95)*

☐ **THE LOVERS' GUIDE TO SENSUOUS ASTROLOGY by Marlowe and Urna Gray.** Let your love sign show you the way, and you'll discover more sensuous variations than you thought it was possible to know in a book that turns perfect strangers into ideal lovers. You'll wonder how you ever loved without it! (123646—$2.95)

☐ **STRANGE SEA STORIES AND LEGENDS by Bill Wisner.** A unique collection that even the most dedicated landlubber will find irresistible reading. From ghost ships and cannibalism, to dashing pirates and man-eating sharks, here are true-life adventures and the incredible lore of the sea. (123581—$3.50)

☐ **INCREDIBLE COINCIDENCE by Alan Vaughan.** The sex novel that mirrored the Patty hearst kidnapping—two years before it happened! ... The woman who discovered the ring she lost forty years before—in a potato! ... and over 150 authentic cases that form evidence that coincidence is more than mere chance, and that it represents a vital clue to psychic powers we are only beginning to understand. (135512—$3.50)*

*Prices slightly higher in Canada

**Buy them at your local
bookstore or use coupon
on last page for ordering.**

All About the Occult from SIGNET

(0451)

☐ **THE COMPLETE BOOK OF MAGIC AND WITCHCRAFT by Kathryn Paulsen.**
Revised edition. An up-to-date practitioner's manual of magic, witchcraft
and sorcery—with all the ancient and modern recipes, spells, and
incantations essential to the Black Arts!   (137361—$3.95)*

☐ **MANY MANSIONS by Gina Cerminara. Introduction by Hugh Lynn Cayce.**
"The Edgar Cayce story on reincarnation," this is the account of the man
and his incredible healing power. The author tells how Cayce saw past
the barriers of space and time, how he penetrated the "previous" lives
of his subjects, and performed the fantastic cures and prophecies that
made him the most remarkable clairvoyant in modern history.
                                                     (137388—$3.50)*

☐ **THE WORLD ALMANAC® BOOK OF THE STRANGE by the Editors of** *The
World Almanac.*® This volume will give you the fullest, most factual
information available on every mysterious being, object, power and event
that has excited your interest and curiosity.   (118928—$3.50)*

☐ **THE WORLD ALMANAC® BOOK OF THE STRANGE #2 by the Editors of** *The
World Almanac.*® The book that travels into the strangest corners and
most hidden depths of the world we live in, as it reveals the most
unexplained and inexplicable events that have ever boggled the human
mind. It will hold you startled, spellbound, and covinced from the first
amazing page to the last.   (118901—$3.50)*

*Prices slightly higher in Canada

Buy them at your local
bookstore or use coupon
on next page for ordering.

⊘ **SIGNET** (0451)

FIND THE ANSWERS!

☐ **ENCYCLOPEDIA OF AMAZING BUT TRUE FACTS by Doug Stover.** Fantastic events, fascinating people, unusual animals—all gathered together in an around-the-world collection that ranges from the bizarre to the miraculous. Complete with over 200 incredible photos. (115597—$3.50)

☐ **HOW TO KNOW THE BIRDS by Roger Tory Peterson.** Here is an authoritative, on-the-spot guide to help you recognize instantly most American birds on sight. Includes a 24-page color supplement. (129393—$4.50)

☐ **HOW INTELLIGENT ARE YOU? by Victor Serebriakoff.** Test your own I.Q. with this series of stimulating tests that can be taken individually or in competitive group participation—all of them with answers and a key to interpreting your scores. (142926—$2.95)

☐ **THE AMATEUR MAGICIAN'S HANDBOOK by Henry Hay.** Fourth revised edition. A professional magician teaches you hundreds of the tricks of his trade in this unsurpassed, illustrated guide. (122569—$3.95)

Prices slightly higher in Canada

Buy them at your local bookstore or use this convenient coupon for ordering.

NEW AMERICAN LIBRARY,
P.O. Box 999, Bergenfield, New Jersey 07621

Please send me the books I have checked above. I am enclosing $_____
(please add $1.00 to this order to cover postage and handling). Send check or money order—no cash or C.O.D.'s. Prices and numbers are subject to change without notice.

Name_____

Address_____

City_____State_____Zip Code_____
Allow 4-6 weeks for delivery.
This offer is subject to withdrawal without notice.